ELECTRIC MINDS

ADHD SUPERPOWERS IN A DISTRACTED WORLD

ELECTRIC MINDS

DR. JOSEPH PAGANO
INTERNATIONAL BESTSELLER & PULITZER PRIZE CONTENDER

Book Cover: Dr. Joseph Pagano

Book Publicists: Samantha Showman & Jodie Pagano, MSW,CRS

Electric Minds

ADHD Superpowers in a Distracted World

Interior formatting by 100 Covers.

First Edition

Paperback ISBN: 979-8-234-13727-2

Hardback ISBN: 979-8-234-14619-9

Primary Influences, Research, & Source Material ⚡

This work was influenced by a combination of:

- neuroscience research,
- trauma-informed perspectives,
- addiction and recovery literature,
- clinical social work principles,
- ADHD advocacy,
- emerging neurodiversity research,
- lived experience narratives,
- and direct interviews and observational insights collected by the author.

Primary texts, researchers, organizations, and influences include:

- — Gabor Maté
- — Edward M. Hallowell & John J. Ratey
- — Ned Hallowell & John Ratey
- — Russell A. Barkley
- — Thomas E. Brown
- — Sari Solden
- — Daniel G. Amen
- — Ari Tuckman
- — Kathleen G. Nadeau
- — Bessel van der Kolk

- — Dr. Joseph Pagano
- Clinical and recovery-oriented perspectives shared through the work and mentorship of Scott Cook, MD, MPH
- Current ADHD, neuroscience, and mental health education resources produced by BrainMD
- Educational and advocacy content provided through The Upside of ADHD
- Emerging literature and public discourse surrounding:
  - emotional dysregulation,
  - Rejection Sensitivity Dysphoria (RSD),
  - trauma overlap,
  - executive dysfunction,
  - neuroplasticity,
  - addiction neuroscience,
  - psychedelic-assisted therapy,
  - nervous system regulation,
  - and neurodiversity-informed treatment approaches.

Additional inspiration and perspective were drawn from:

- lived experiences shared anonymously by individuals with ADHD across diverse racial, cultural, socioeconomic, recovery, and professional backgrounds,
- conversations with parents, educators, clinicians, recovering individuals, and advocates,
- the author's direct clinical experience in behavioral health and recovery-oriented systems,
- and years of observing the emotional impact of untreated or misunderstood ADHD in both children and adults.

This book represents an intersection of science, storytelling, advocacy, lived experience, and human emotion intended to challenge shame and create greater understanding surrounding ADHD and neurodivergence.

“Electric minds were never meant to be shamed into silence.” ⚡

AUTHOR'S NOTE

This book was never written to romanticize ADHD.

It was also never written to reduce ADHD to a trendy social media label, a punchline, or a collection of "quirky" personality traits.

This book was written because behind millions of people diagnosed with ADHD are nervous systems that have spent years trying to survive overwhelm, shame, emotional intensity, misunderstanding, and exhaustion.

Some people with ADHD build extraordinary lives while privately battling chaos no one else can see.

Some quietly drown beneath burnout, anxiety, addiction, rejection sensitivity, impulsivity, emotional dysregulation, and the constant feeling of being "too much."

Others spend decades believing they are lazy, broken, dramatic, weak, or failing at life, when in reality, they have been trying to function inside nervous systems that processed the world differently from the very beginning.

This book is deeply personal.

Parts of these chapters come directly from Dr. Joey Pagano's own life experiences as:

- a child diagnosed with ADHD,
- a person in long-term recovery,
- a clinician,
- an educator,
- a husband and father,
- and someone who spent years trying to understand the chaos inside his own mind.

At the same time, this book was also shaped by the voices of others: children, parents, professionals, recovering addicts, high-functioning adults, women who masked their symptoms for decades, and individuals who shared their lived experiences so others might finally feel understood.

Some stories have been adapted, anonymized, or reconstructed to protect privacy while preserving emotional truth and clinical relevance.

This book blends:

- neuroscience,
- psychology,
- trauma-informed perspectives,
- clinical experience,
- lived experience,
- and emerging conversations surrounding neurodivergence, emotional regulation, addiction, burnout, and modern overstimulation.

It is not intended to replace medical advice, psychiatric care, therapy, or individualized treatment.

Instead, its purpose is something much more human:

To help people feel seen.

To reduce shame.

To create understanding.

To challenge outdated narratives.

And to remind every person with an electric mind that struggling does not mean they are broken.

Because sometimes the people who feel the most overwhelmed internally are also the ones carrying the most unrecognized brilliance within them.

And maybe understanding that changes everything.

DEDICATION

To every child who was told to "calm down" when their nervous system was begging to be understood.

To every adult who spent years believing they were lazy, broken, too emotional, too intense, or too much.

To the exhausted parents trying their best to raise children whose minds move faster than the world around them.

To the teachers, clinicians, advocates, and caregivers who choose compassion instead of shame.

To those silently battling addiction, burnout, anxiety, emotional overwhelm, and the crushing weight of masking who they truly are just to survive.

To the people who never felt understood until someone finally gave a name to the chaos inside their minds.

And most importantly, to every person with an electric mind who survived long enough to realize they were never broken in the first place.

This book is for you. ⚡

Table of Contents

PROLOGUE

Too Much, Too Fast

I remember the holidays before I remember understanding myself.

That is the strange thing about ADHD.

Long before I ever heard the words *attention deficit hyperactivity disorder,* before doctors, report cards, behavior charts, and medication bottles entered my life—I already knew one thing: Something about me was different.

I did not have language for it back then.

I only had feelings.

Big feelings.

Feelings that were too big.

The kind that filled my entire body until I thought I might burst from the inside out.

I remember Thanksgiving in 1983 more clearly than I probably should.

I was eight years old.

The house was loud before the sun had fully come up.

I remember waking early because my brain almost never let me sleep deeply before holidays. Excitement felt too intense. It felt overwhelming. My thoughts began racing the second my eyes opened.

Thanksgiving felt enormous to me.

Everything did.

I remember lying in bed, staring at the ceiling while my thoughts sprinted ahead of the day.

Who was coming over?

Would there be pumpkin pie?

Would my cousins be there?

Would somebody yell today?

Would I get in trouble again?

Would I accidentally say something stupid?

Would everybody else somehow know how to act normal while I spent another holiday trying to force myself not to feel like electricity?

That was one of the hardest parts of growing up with ADHD before anyone understood what was happening inside me.

I was constantly aware that other people seemed able to move naturally through environments that overwhelmed me. They could sit at the table, answer questions, laugh at the right moments, and shift from one conversation to another as if their bodies knew exactly what to do. I watched them and tried to copy it. But inside, I felt like I was working ten times harder just to appear calm.

I noticed everything.

Every sound.

Every emotional shift.

Every facial expression.

Every change in tone.

Every tension in the room.

Even at eight years old, my nervous system never seemed to rest. It was as if my body was always searching for danger, even when nothing dangerous was actually happening. I did not know how to explain it then. I only knew that my body reacted before my mind had time to understand why.

I remember hearing pots and pans clattering in the kitchen before I even got out of bed.

The smell of turkey drifted down the hallway.

Coffee. Butter. Cigarette smoke.

The sharp smell of cleaning products my mother used while getting the house ready for company.

The sensory experience of holidays felt gigantic.

Most people probably remember holidays through moments and memories.

I remember them through nervous system reactions.

The brightness of the lights.

The texture of my clothes.

The sound of football blaring from the television.

The pressure of adults asking questions.

The anticipation.

The overstimulation.

The emotional intensity.

It all felt too close.

My mother, Cindy, moved quickly through the house, trying to get everything ready before family arrived.

I can still hear the cabinet doors slamming.

I can still hear the adults saying:

"Joey, settle down."

"Joey, stop running."

"Joey, stop touching everything."

"Joey, calm down."

The strange thing was, I wanted to.

That is what so many people misunderstand about children with ADHD.

People often assume we are being intentionally difficult.

Most of us are trying harder than anyone can see.

I was trying.

I remember trying to force my body to stay still.

Trying to keep my legs steady.

Trying not to interrupt.

Trying not to blurt things out.

Trying not to get too excited.

But excitement did not feel like something I could control.

That's what ADHD often felt like for me as a child.

Not a lack of caring.

A lack of brakes.

My brain moved too fast.

My emotions moved too fast.

My body moved too fast.

And by the time I recognized the overwhelm, it had already taken over.

I remember standing in the kitchen while adults talked around me.

Someone laughed loudly.

A football announcer yelled from the television.

The oven timer beeped.

Someone dropped silverware into the sink.

The dog barked.

My cousins ran through the living room.

Every single sound hit my nervous system individually.

That is something people who do not live with ADHD often struggle to understand.

The ADHD nervous system often processes stimulation differently.

What feels manageable to one person can feel emotionally exhausting to another. And when stimulation builds faster than regulation, the nervous system eventually crashes.

But before the crash comes the hyperactivity.

The emotional acceleration.

The feeling of almost vibrating inside your own skin.

That is how holidays felt to me.

I would become louder.

Faster.

More impulsive.

More emotional.

Not because I was trying to ruin anything.

Because my nervous system was overloaded.

I remember running through the hallway while adults prepared dinner.

I remember talking too much.

I remember interrupting constantly because thoughts entered my head with such intensity that keeping them inside felt impossible.

People with ADHD often describe their thoughts as racing.

That word never fully captured it for me.

It felt more like my brain had no filter for everything coming in.

Thoughts crashed into each other.

Ideas overlapped.

Sounds blended together.

Memories surfaced without warning.

Questions exploded in my mind.

Even as a child, silence almost never existed inside my head.

I remember trying to explain things and getting frustrated because my mouth could never move as fast as my thoughts.

Adults would say:

"Slow down."

But slowing down felt impossible.

Like trying to stop a train with my bare hands.

I remember sitting at the Thanksgiving table, trying harder than anyone around me could see.

The food looked beautiful.

Turkey. Stuffing. Mashed potatoes. Corn. Rolls.

Pumpkin pie waiting off to the side for later.

Everyone else seemed calm.

Meanwhile, my leg bounced violently beneath the table.

The tablecloth moved with it.

I remember pressing my hands against my leg, trying to make it stop.

That is the part people don't see. The effort.

Children with ADHD often spend enormous amounts of energy trying not to be themselves.

Trying not to move.

Trying not to interrupt.

Trying not to react too strongly.

Trying not to disappoint anyone.

Eventually, something happened.

It always did.

I don't remember exactly what I said.

I only remember the feeling afterward.

I interrupted someone.

Probably loudly.

Probably impulsively.

Probably without realizing it.

The room shifted.

The adults stopped talking. And then came the look.

That look… the disappointed look.

For children with ADHD, disappointment can feel catastrophic.

Not because we are weak.

But because many of us feel emotional responses with overwhelming intensity.

Today, clinicians understand much more about emotional dysregulation, rejection sensitivity dysphoria, executive dysfunction, and nervous system activation.

Back then, people mostly saw behavior.

And my behavior always seemed to be the problem.

I remember heat rushing into my chest.

I remember staring down at my plate, pretending not to care.

I remember embarrassment so intense it almost felt physical.

That feeling stayed with me for hours.

That is another thing people often fail to understand about ADHD.

We don't simply experience moments.

We replay them. Over and over.

The criticism.

The awkward interaction.

The disappointment.

The correction.

The look on someone's face.

The sentence we wish we could take back.

The moment we realized we had done it again.

Many people with ADHD carry emotional experiences long after everyone else has moved on. What may seem like a small correction to someone else can become an entire internal story for us.

I remember sitting there, trying to disappear inside myself.

That shift happened constantly in childhood.

One moment, I was excited.

The next, I felt ashamed for existing too loudly.

That emotional whiplash became normal.

And over time, I started to believe something was fundamentally wrong with me.

Not because anyone explicitly said it.

Because repeated correction slowly teaches children that they are difficult.

And eventually, difficult children can become adults who privately believe they are burdens.

I carried that feeling everywhere.

Into classrooms.

Into friendships.

Into relationships.

Into addiction.

Especially addiction.

Because years later, when substances finally slowed my brain down, when the noise grew quieter for the first time, it made emotional sense to me.

That is something society often misunderstands about addiction and ADHD.

Many people with ADHD are not simply chasing pleasure.

Many are chasing relief.

Relief from overstimulation.

Relief from emotional flooding.

Relief from shame.

Relief from the exhausting speed of their own thoughts.

Even as a child, I constantly felt emotionally drained from trying to regulate myself.

And yet, despite all the difficulty, there were also beautiful things happening inside my mind.

I was deeply imaginative.

Curious.

Emotionally intuitive.

Creative.

Passionate.

I noticed patterns quickly.

I asked questions constantly.

I could become completely absorbed in ideas.

I could feel empathy intensely.

But nobody knew how to nurture those qualities yet.

So instead, most adults focused on controlling the parts of me that seemed disruptive. And to be fair, they were doing the best they could with the understanding they had.

In the early 1980s, ADHD awareness looked very different from what it does today.

People talked about hyperactive boys.

They rarely talked about:

- emotional regulation
- rejection sensitivity
- nervous system overload
- sensory overwhelm
- dopamine dysregulation
- trauma overlap
- executive dysfunction

The public understanding was shallow.

Children like me were often labeled as:

"too emotional"

"too sensitive"

"too hyper"

"too much"

That phrase stayed with me.

Too much. Too loud. Too fast. Too emotional. Too impulsive. Too intense.

And honestly, intensity may be one of the most defining characteristics of ADHD.

Many of us do not experience life halfway.

We feel deeply. We think rapidly. We love intensely. We react emotionally. We become consumed by interests. We chase stimulation. We crash hard.

Our nervous systems often operate at extremes.

That intensity can become extraordinary when it is properly understood.

It can also become destructive when it is misunderstood.

At eight years old, I understood none of this.

I only knew that holidays left me emotionally exhausted.

I remember lying awake later that night, replaying the entire day in my mind.

Every interaction. Every embarrassing moment. Every correction. Every feeling.

My brain never stopped.

That was one of the loneliest parts of childhood.

People assumed the moment was over.

But inside me, it kept going.

That is the hidden reality many children with ADHD carry.

The emotional experience doesn't end when the event ends.

The nervous system keeps reliving it.

That's why shame becomes so deeply wired into many ADHD identities.

Not because ADHD itself creates shame.

Because repeated misunderstanding does.

Eventually, around age ten, I was diagnosed with ADHD.

Suddenly, there was a name for what adults had spent years trying to control.

Medication entered the picture.

Ritalin.

School meetings.

Behavior conversations.

Adults discussed me instead of understanding me.

And while medication absolutely helped in some ways, it did not magically erase the emotional scars that had already begun to form.

It didn't teach emotional regulation.

It didn't explain why rejection felt devastating.

It didn't explain why my nervous system constantly searched for stimulation.

It didn't explain why simply existing could feel emotionally exhausting.

That understanding would take decades.

And some of it would come through enormous pain.

Because untreated or misunderstood ADHD doesn't disappear. It evolves.

The child who couldn't regulate emotions becomes the overwhelmed adult.

The child constantly seeking stimulation becomes the adult more vulnerable to addiction.

The child terrified of disappointing people becomes the adult trapped in perfectionism, people-pleasing, burnout, and emotional masking.

But there is another side to the story.

Inside many ADHD minds, there is extraordinary potential.

Creativity.

Empathy.

Innovation.

Intensity.

Passion.

Resilience.

The same nervous system that creates chaos can also create brilliance.

That's the paradox.

ADHD can feel like carrying both a superpower and a wound inside the same brain.

This book exists because millions of people are silently living inside that contradiction.

Children.

Teenagers.

Parents.

Professionals.

Recovering addicts.

Executives.

Creators.

People who look successful on the outside while privately feeling exhausted.

People who have spent their lives believing they were broken.

I know that feeling intimately.

But over time, I learned something important.

The goal is not to destroy the electric mind.

The goal is to understand it.

To regulate it.

To work with it.

To stop seeing yourself as defective simply because your nervous system experiences the world differently.

Because once you finally understand what ADHD actually is, and once you stop reducing it to stereotypes about distraction and hyperactivity, you begin to realize something powerful.

You were never weak.

You were carrying an overwhelming amount of emotional electricity inside a nervous system nobody taught you how to regulate.

And for many people reading this book, that realization changes everything.

PART I

THE STORM BEFORE THE DIAGNOSIS

CHAPTER ONE

The Holidays Were Always Loud

The strange thing about childhood ADHD is that you often sense you are different long before you understand why.

Before the diagnosis.

Before medication.

Before teachers start using words like *disruptive.*

Before adults begin holding meetings about your behavior.

You already feel it.

You feel it when your emotions rise faster than everyone else's.

You feel it when excitement somehow turns into trouble.

You feel it when adults look exhausted by behaviors you do not fully understand yourself.

And most painfully, you feel it everytime you realize other people seem able to control things inside themselves that you cannot.

As a child, I constantly felt as if life moved too fast for my nervous system.

Not just holidays. Everything.

School.

Birthday parties.

Family gatherings.

Church.

Restaurants.

Little League games.

Even ordinary conversations.

My brain absorbed everything around me at once.

The fluorescent lights in classrooms.

The pencils tapping against desks.

The whispers from other students.

The scrape of chairs across the floor.

The ticking clock.

The slight shift in a teacher's tone when frustration crept in.

Most people do not realize how exhausting it can be when your nervous system cannot filter stimulation the way others seem to.

By the time I was eight years old, I was already tired.

Not physically tired, but emotionally tired.

There is a difference.

Physical exhaustion lets you rest.

ADHD exhaustion can keep your brain awake long after the world has gone quiet, replaying everything you said, everything you missed, every look on someone's face, and every moment you wish you could redo.

◈

Too Excited to Sit Still

I remember being terrified of getting in trouble while also being unable to stop doing the very things that got me in trouble.

That contradiction shaped almost my entire childhood.

I wanted to behave.

I wanted adults to be proud of me.

I wanted teachers to like me.

I wanted my parents to stop looking stressed every time my name was mentioned.

But wanting to regulate myself and being able to regulate myself were two entirely different things.

That is one of the greatest misunderstandings about ADHD.

People often assume behavior is purely a choice.

But ADHD frequently affects the brain's ability to regulate impulses, emotions, attention, timing, stimulation, and executive functioning.

As a child, I did not understand any of that scientifically.

I only knew that every day felt like trying to hold the steering wheel while my brain accelerated faster than I could control.

I remember school being one of the hardest places emotionally.

Not because I wasn't intelligent.

Actually, intelligence became part of the confusion.

Teachers would often say things like:

"Joey is smart."

"He knows the material."

"He has so much potential."

And then, almost immediately after:

"But he doesn't focus."

"He talks constantly."

"He gets distracted."

"He cannot stay seated."

"He interrupts."

"He rushes through his work."

That inconsistency became part of my identity.

I was bright enough for adults to expect more from me, but dysregulated enough that I constantly struggled to meet those expectations.

That creates enormous shame in children.

Because when people believe you are capable, but your executive functioning repeatedly collapses under pressure, you eventually begin to feel as if you are failing on purpose.

◈

Every Sound Felt Bigger

I remember sitting in classrooms, trying desperately to focus while my mind drifted in every direction imaginable.

A bird outside the window.

The sound of someone coughing.

The way sunlight hit the floor.

A random thought about a television show.

An idea for something funny.

The feeling of my sock bunching inside my shoe.

The anxiety of wondering whether the teacher was upset with me.

Then, suddenly, I would realize several minutes had passed, and I had no idea what was happening in class anymore.

People often describe ADHD as an attention problem.

But for many of us, attention was never absent.

Attention was everywhere.

The problem was not that I could not pay attention.

The problem was that my brain struggled to decide what deserved attention first.

Everything felt equally loud.

Every sound.

Every thought.

Every sensation.

Every emotion.

It was exhausting.

And because no one could physically see what was happening inside my nervous system, adults often interpreted my struggles as laziness, defiance, immaturity, or lack of discipline.

I remember getting yelled at for things I genuinely forgot.

Homework.

Folders.

Jackets.

Assignments.

Instructions.

People assumed forgetting meant not caring.

But ADHD forgetfulness often has nothing to do with caring.

In fact, many people with ADHD care so intensely that forgetting something can create overwhelming guilt.

◈

The Look

I remember panic.

Real panic.

The kind that hit when a teacher asked for an assignment I had forgotten at home.

The embarrassment.

The adrenaline.

The shame.

The fear of disappointing people.

Children with ADHD often experience life through a series of micro-failures.

Small mistakes.

Small corrections.

Small disappointments.

Over time, those moments stack inside you.

People only see the missing homework.

They don't see the internal collapse that happens afterward.

I remember going home after difficult school days and replaying every interaction in my mind.

Every correction.

Every embarrassing moment.

Every time classmates laughed.

Every time a teacher sounded frustrated.

Even the smallest moments felt enormous.

That emotional intensity became one of the defining characteristics of my childhood.

I did not just feel emotions. I became them.

Excitement consumed me.

Embarrassment consumed me.

Shame consumed me.

Anger consumed me.

There was no emotional volume control.

Everything happened at full intensity.

Today, clinicians recognize emotional dysregulation as a major component of ADHD.

Back then, it was rarely discussed.

Adults simply saw overreactions.

But internally, it felt like my nervous system was constantly flooding.

One criticism could ruin my entire day.

One disappointed look could replay in my head for hours.

One embarrassing moment at school consume me all night.

And because I felt everything so deeply, I became hyperaware of rejection.

I could sense mood changes instantly.

A teacher's tone.

My father's irritation.

Someone laughing after I spoke.

Feeling left out.

Feeling corrected.

Feeling misunderstood.

Even before rejection sensitivity dysphoria had a name, I was already living inside it.

◈

The Punishment Cycle

The problem was that no one around me understood the emotional intensity beneath my behavior.

They saw movement.

Noise.

Interruptions.

Impulsivity.

They didn't see the exhaustion underneath it all.

I remember church being especially difficult.

The expectation to sit still and stay quiet felt almost unbearable.

The harder I tried not to move, the more aware I became of every sensation in my body.

My legs bounced.

My thoughts raced.

My attention wandered.

Then came the correction.

A whisper.

A look.

A hand on my shoulder telling me to calm down.

And immediately, shame flooded through me.

That cycle repeated throughout childhood.

Excitement.

Impulsivity.

Correction.

Shame.

Overthinking.

Trying harder.

Repeating the same behavior.

Over and over.

People often ask why so many adults with ADHD struggle with self-esteem.

The answer often begins in childhood.

When children repeatedly receive the message that behaviors tied to their nervous system are wrong, they begin to internalize the belief that something about them is defective.

I know I did.

I spent years believing I was failing at being normal.

The confusing part was that I often excelled in certain areas.

When something interested me, I could become completely consumed by it.

Obsessed.

Hyperfocused.

Hours disappeared.

I could memorize information quickly.

I could be creative.

I could think outside the box.

I could feel emotionally connected to ideas in ways other people sometimes did not.

But the same brain capable of extraordinary focus under the right stimulation could collapse under tasks that felt boring, repetitive, emotionally overwhelming, or unstimulating.

That inconsistency confused adults. Honestly, it confused me too.

◈

Trying to Be Normal

How could I focus so intensely on some things and struggle so completely with others?

Why did simple tasks feel impossible on certain days?

Why could I become consumed by an interest and still forget basic responsibilities?

Today, we understand much more about dopamine regulation, reward circuitry, executive functioning, and ADHD neuroscience.

But back then, it mostly felt like I was disappointing people no matter how hard I tried not to.

I remember report cards becoming emotional events.

Teachers described me as:

"Bright but distracted."

"Capable but inconsistent."

"Talkative."

"Needs better self-control."

What no one recognized was that every one of those comments became part of how I saw myself.

Children absorb language.

Especially repeated language.

And eventually, repeated criticism begins to harden into identity.

One of the most painful parts of ADHD is that many children begin connecting their natural nervous system to failure long before they understand what ADHD actually is.

I remember trying to explain myself and not knowing how.

How do you explain to adults that your brain feels too loud?

How do you explain that you are trying?

How do you explain that your emotions feel physically overwhelming?

How do you explain that excitement itself can become painful when your nervous system cannot regulate it?

At eight years old, I didn't have those words.

I only had behaviors.

And behaviors are easy to judge when no one understands the nervous system beneath them.

That misunderstanding followed me everywhere.

Family gatherings.

School.

Friendships.

Sports.

Church.

Public places.

I always felt like I was one emotional reaction away from disappointing someone.

That kind of pressure creates hypervigilance in children.

You start scanning constantly.

Watching faces.

Watching reactions.

Trying to figure out whether people are frustrated with you.

That emotional hyperawareness stayed with me into adulthood.

And honestly, it became one of the hidden engines behind both my empathy and my anxiety.

◈

Smart Enough to Know Something Was Wrong

Many people with ADHD become deeply emotionally perceptive because their nervous systems spend years monitoring environments for signs of criticism, rejection, or emotional change.

That sensitivity can become a strength.

It can also become exhausting.

I remember feeling emotionally drained after social situations while other children seemed unaffected.

It wasn't because I disliked people.

It was because my nervous system absorbed everything.

The noise.

The emotions.

The stimulation.

The pressure.

The fear of getting in trouble.

Everything stayed with me.

And underneath all of it was confusion.

Why was everything so hard?

Why did simple things feel overwhelming?

Why did adults keep telling me to calm down when my body felt incapable of calming down?

That confusion eventually became frustration.

And frustration eventually became anger.

Not because I wanted to be angry.

Because emotional exhaustion can eventually turn into emotional volatility.

That's another misunderstood part of ADHD.

Many emotional reactions are not manipulation.

They are overwhelmed nervous systems reaching capacity.

As I got older, I began discovering things that could quiet my brain for a while.

Excitement.

Chaos.

Risk.

Eventually, substances.

That connection between ADHD and addiction is deeply important.

Because many individuals with ADHD are not simply impulsive.

Many are desperately searching for regulation.

Anything that slows the noise.

Anything that numbs the emotional overload.

Anything that creates temporary calm.

That search can become dangerous quickly.

But before addiction ever entered my life, the emotional groundwork was already there.

◈

The Storm Before the Diagnosis

The shame.

The overstimulation.

The emotional flooding.

The rejection sensitivity.

The constant feeling that I was somehow failing, even though I was trying harder than people realized.

Eventually, around age ten, I was diagnosed with ADHD.

Suddenly, adults had a label.

Medication conversations began.

Ritalin entered my life.

Teachers saw me differently.

Parents saw me differently.

I saw myself differently.

Part of me felt relieved. Part of me felt defective.

That complexity matters.

Because a diagnosis can be both validating and painful at the same time.

On one hand, there is finally an explanation.

On the other hand, many children internalize diagnosis as proof that something is "wrong" with them.

That was especially true in the 1980s and early 1990s, when ADHD stigma was intense.

Kids were often labeled:

Hyper.

Problematic.

Medicated.

Out of control.

There was very little public understanding of the emotional reality beneath ADHD.

Very little understanding of nervous systems.

Very little understanding of trauma overlap.

Very little understanding of rejection sensitivity.

Most conversations focused on controlling behavior.

Not understanding the child.

And that distinction matters.

Because children do not heal through shame.

They heal through understanding.

Looking back now, I can see that so much of my childhood behavior wasn't rebellion.

It was dysregulation.

It was an overloaded nervous system trying desperately to survive environments it could not fully process.

And yet, inside that same nervous system existed enormous potential.

Creativity.

Empathy.

Passion.

Intensity.

Curiosity.

Resilience.

The same mind that created chaos also created possibility.

That's what makes ADHD so complicated.

It can feel like both a superpower and a wound.

A gift and an exhaustion.

A brilliant mind inside a nervous system still learning how to regulate itself.

That was the storm before the diagnosis.

And for millions of people reading this book, that storm never fully ended.

It simply grew older with them.

CHAPTER TWO

The Dopamine Hunter ⚡

Chaos, Urgency, Overstimulation, and the ADHD Brain's Search for Relief

◈

Chaos Felt Normal

The first thing most people misunderstand about ADHD is this:

People with ADHD are not always seeking attention.

Many are seeking stimulation.

That distinction changes everything.

By the time Joseph reached adolescence, his nervous system had already spent years caught between two emotional extremes:

- overwhelm
- under-stimulation

Everything felt too loud emotionally, until suddenly, nothing felt loud enough.

And when the ADHD brain becomes under-stimulated, something dangerous can begin to happen internally:

The nervous system starts hunting.

Hunting for:

- urgency
- novelty

- excitement
- intensity
- risk
- emotional activation
- dopamine

The ADHD brain can crave movement the way starving lungs crave oxygen.

Not because the person is weak.

Because the nervous system is trying desperately to regulate itself.

That is why many people with ADHD unconsciously create chaos around themselves without realizing it.

Chaos creates stimulation.

Deadlines create stimulation.

Conflict creates stimulation.

Risk creates stimulation.

Novelty creates stimulation.

Even emotional pain can become neurologically stimulating over time, especially when calmness feels unfamiliar.

Joseph did not understand any of this growing up.

He only knew that stillness felt unbearable.

Silence felt uncomfortable.

And boredom?

Boredom felt physically painful.

Not metaphorically painful.

Physically painful.

That is one of the realities many people without ADHD struggle to understand:

For some ADHD nervous systems, boredom does not feel neutral.

It feels agitating. Almost threatening.

The brain begins searching for something that can raise stimulation again.

Anything.

Music.

Television.

Movement.

Humor.

Talking.

Arguments.

Video games.

Risk.

Social media.

Food.

Sex.

Shopping.

Substances.

The object changes.

The neurological search remains the same.

◈

Why Boredom Hurt

As a child, Joseph constantly heard adults say things like:

"Just sit still."

"Relax."

"Slow down."

"Why are you always doing something?"

But his nervous system never experienced inactivity the way other people seemed to.

Inactivity did not feel restful.

It felt emotionally itchy.

Like energy trapped beneath the skin.

Like thoughts colliding faster than he could organize them.

Like his brain was revving inside him with nowhere for the energy to go.

This is one reason many people with ADHD struggle profoundly in environments that require:

- repetitive tasks
- low stimulation
- prolonged sitting
- delayed reward
- passive learning

The ADHD nervous system often struggles with dopamine regulation, especially in areas involving motivation and reward.

Research on ADHD increasingly points toward differences involving:

- dopamine transmission
- reward anticipation
- executive functioning
- motivation circuitry
- novelty response

That matters because dopamine is not simply the "pleasure chemical" people casually describe online.

Dopamine plays major roles in:

- motivation
- anticipation
- attention
- reinforcement
- reward-seeking
- engagement
- behavioral activation

For many individuals with ADHD, the brain constantly searches for enough stimulation to feel emotionally and cognitively "awake."

And when healthy stimulation is unavailable, the nervous system may begin seeking unhealthy stimulation instead.

◈

The Addiction to Urgency

Joseph became addicted to urgency long before he became addicted to substances.

Urgency created focus.

Deadlines created adrenaline.

Pressure created temporary clarity.

Without urgency, tasks felt impossible to start.

With urgency, his brain suddenly activated.

That pattern follows countless adults with ADHD throughout life.

They procrastinate.

Avoid.

Delay.

Freeze.

Then, suddenly, they complete massive amounts of work under extreme pressure.

Outsiders often misunderstand this cycle.

They assume laziness.

Lack of discipline.

Poor motivation.

But internally, the ADHD nervous system may be waiting desperately for enough stimulation to activate executive functioning.

That is one reason many people with ADHD become:

- chronic procrastinators

- adrenaline seekers
- crisis managers
- high-pressure performers

The chaos itself becomes neurologically reinforcing.

Joseph saw this pattern everywhere in his own life.

Especially academically.

He was intelligent.

Teachers knew it.

Family members knew it.

But assignments often remained untouched until panic arrived.

Then, suddenly:

- focus appeared
- energy appeared
- urgency appeared
- productivity exploded

That inconsistency created enormous shame.

Because from the outside, it looked like:

"He only applies himself when he wants to."

But internally, it felt more like:

"Why can't I access this level of functioning consistently?"

That question haunted him.

And it continues to haunt millions of adults with ADHD today.

◈

Dopamine on Demand

As Joseph got older, the world around him became increasingly engineered for dopamine delivery.

Fast television.

Video games.

Constant entertainment.

Eventually:

- smartphones
- social media
- notifications
- scrolling
- instant gratification

Modern technology learned how to monetize overstimulated nervous systems.

Especially ADHD nervous systems.

Apps became dopamine machines.

Refresh.

Scroll.

Notification.

Reward.

Repeat.

The brain learns quickly:

"Stimulation is always available."

For people with ADHD who already struggle with dopamine regulation, that loop can become incredibly powerful.

Social media platforms understand this well.

They are built around:

- unpredictability
- novelty
- emotional activation
- rapid reward cycles

The same nervous system that struggles to focus during low-stimulation tasks may suddenly hyperfocus for hours in stimulation-rich environments.

That contradiction confuses many people.

"How can someone with ADHD focus on TikTok for four hours but not answer one email?"

Because ADHD is not always a lack of attention.

Often, it is a dysregulation of attention.

The ADHD brain does not consistently choose attention based on importance.

It often follows stimulation.

That distinction matters enormously.

◈

The Brain That Couldn't Slow Down

Nighttime became especially difficult.

The world grew quieter outside, but louder inside.

Many people with ADHD describe nighttime as the moment the brain becomes impossible to escape.

Thoughts race.

Memories replay.

Conversations rewind.

Ideas multiply.

Anxiety increases

Regret resurfaces.

The nervous system stays active long after the body is exhausted.

Joseph experienced this constantly.

Especially during adolescence, emotional stress, and periods of shame.

His mind became relentless.

And without understanding ADHD neurologically, he took those experiences personally.

Weakness.

Failure.

Brokenness.

He began asking himself:

"Why can't I just shut my brain off like everybody else?"

That question would eventually shape many of his later struggles with:

- anxiety
- emotional dysregulation
- addiction
- burnout
- nervous system exhaustion

Because eventually, he discovered something terrifying:

Substances quieted the noise.

At least temporarily.

◈

Searching for Stimulation

This is one of the most important truths society still misunderstands about ADHD:

Many people are not seeking destruction.

They are seeking regulation.

Unfortunately, the nervous system often cannot tell the difference between:

- healthy stimulation
- unhealthy stimulation

It only knows that stimulation changes internal chemistry.

That is why people with ADHD may become vulnerable to:

- addiction
- compulsive behaviors
- risky behavior
- emotional chaos

- overspending
- binge eating
- toxic relationships
- thrill-seeking
- social media dependency

The object changes.

The neurological pursuit remains remarkably similar.

Joseph recognized this pattern only much later in life.

Especially in recovery.

Because once substances disappeared, the nervous system still demanded stimulation.

The brain still moved rapidly.

The emotional intensity remained.

The restlessness still existed.

Everything substances had temporarily numbed came rushing back.

At first, that realization felt overwhelming.

Eventually, it also became clarifying.

Because healing required more than sobriety.

It required understanding the nervous system.

◈

When Calm Felt Uncomfortable

One of the strangest realities for many people with ADHD is this:

Calmness can feel emotionally unsafe.

Not because peace is unwanted.

Because the nervous system has learned to recognize intensity as normal.

People raised inside chaos, overstimulation, emotional unpredictability, and constant urgency often struggle to trust stillness.

Stillness feels unfamiliar.

And unfamiliarity can trigger anxiety.

Joseph eventually realized that he had spent years unconsciously recreating urgency around himself because urgency felt normal.

Without stimulation, his brain felt underpowered.

Without chaos, life sometimes felt flat.

That realization changed the way he understood:

- addiction
- burnout
- relationships
- emotional conflict
- productivity addiction
- overstimulation

Beneath many of those struggles was the same nervous system searching for enough activation to feel regulated.

And perhaps that is one of the most important conversations surrounding ADHD:

People are not simply struggling with attention.

Many are struggling with nervous system regulation in a world that:

- overstimulates them,
- shames them,
- exhausts them,
- and sells them endless dopamine as a way to survive it.

That combination is dangerous.

Especially for emotionally sensitive people.

Especially for traumatized people.

Especially for children.

Especially for recovering addicts.

And yet, inside the same nervous system constantly searching for stimulation, extraordinary potential can also live.

- Creativity.
- Innovation.
- Intuition.
- Emotional depth.
- Resilience.
- Passion.
- Visionary thinking.

The challenge is learning how to channel the electricity without letting it burn everything down.

Because unmanaged stimulation-seeking can destroy lives.

But when that same intensity is understood, regulated, and directed with care, it can build extraordinary ones.

CHAPTER THREE

Gifted, Failing, and Exhausted

Some of the most emotionally exhausted people in the world are high-functioning individuals with ADHD.

Not because they are incapable.

But because they have spent their entire lives learning how to appear capable while quietly falling apart beneath the performance.

That distinction matters.

The world often assumes that success means wellness.

It does not.

Many individuals with ADHD learn early that achievement can become armor.

If they perform well enough...

If they become successful enough...

If they become useful enough...

If they become productive enough...

Maybe no one will notice how difficult everything feels on the inside.

And that creates an invisible crisis among high-functioning adults with ADHD.

The world praises them.

But privately, they are:

- overwhelmed
- emotionally exhausted

- overstimulated
- burned out
- anxious
- constantly masking
- terrified of failure
- terrified of disappointing people

Many of them silently believe that if they ever stop performing, everything around them will collapse.

So fear becomes the fuel.

And eventually, that fuel becomes poison.

◈

You Have So Much Potential

Many children with ADHD grow up hearing the same sentence again and again:

"You have so much potential."

At first, it sounds like encouragement.

Over time, it can begin to feel devastating.

Because eventually, the child starts hearing the sentence that follows, even when no one says it aloud:

You have so much potential, so why can't you get it together?

That contradiction creates enormous shame.

Especially in intelligent children.

Many children with ADHD are creative, emotionally intuitive, verbally gifted, innovative, curious, and capable of intense learning when something truly engages them.

But ADHD often creates inconsistency.

And inconsistency confuses people.

Teachers.

Parents.

Employers.

Even the individuals themselves.

One day, the person performs exceptionally.

The next, they struggle to complete simple tasks.

One moment, they appear brilliant.

The next, they feel unable to organize basic responsibilities.

That unpredictability becomes emotionally exhausting.

Especially when the outside world keeps mistaking executive dysfunction for laziness.

Researchers such as Thomas E. Brown have written extensively about how ADHD involves impairments in executive functioning systems responsible for organization, prioritization, emotional regulation, task initiation, and sustained effort.

That helps explain why so many people with ADHD describe themselves as:

"Smart but overwhelmed."

The issue is rarely intelligence.

The issue is regulation.

But children do not naturally understand neuroscience.

Children understand emotion.

And eventually, many absorb the belief that they are failing at life despite trying harder than anyone realizes.

That belief becomes dangerous.

Because once shame attaches itself to intelligence, people stop seeing themselves as struggling.

They begin seeing themselves as defective.

◈

The Child Who Learned to Perform

Many individuals with ADHD become performers long before adulthood.

Not entertainers.

Survivors.

Children quickly learn which behaviors earn approval and which ones invite rejection.

So they adapt.

Some become:

- hyper-achievers
- perfectionists
- caretakers
- comedians
- athletes
- class clowns
- emotionally invisible
- obsessive workers

Anything to avoid criticism.

Anything to avoid shame.

Anything to avoid being "too much."

That adaptation is often called masking.

And masking can become one of the most psychologically exhausting aspects of high-functioning ADHD.

The child studies:

- tone of voice
- body language
- facial reactions
- timing

- social expectations
- emotional responses

Many children with ADHD become emotionally hyperaware because they have spent years trying not to disappoint people.

That hyperawareness can later become:

- anxiety
- people-pleasing
- overthinking
- rejection sensitivity
- emotional exhaustion

But it can also become:

- empathy
- emotional intelligence
- intuition
- interpersonal awareness

That is the paradox of ADHD.

The same nervous system that creates suffering can also create extraordinary emotional depth.

◈

The Mask of Functioning

Many high-functioning adults with ADHD become experts at psychological performance.

They appear regulated.

Pretending to be organized.

Pretending to feel emotionally stable.

Pretending that they are in control.

The outside world sees:

- achievement

- intelligence
- charisma
- productivity
- leadership
- creativity

But the internal world often tells a different story.

Missed deadlines buried under all-night work sessions.

Chronic anxiety disguised as humor.

Sleep deprivation hidden beneath caffeine.

Emotional flooding hidden beneath professionalism.

Many high-functioning adults with ADHD live in a state of near-constant nervous system overactivation.

And because they continue to function on the outside, few people recognize how dysregulated they feel on the inside.

That invisibility becomes dangerous.

Especially among professionals.

Clinicians.

Executives.

Entrepreneurs.

Educators.

First responders.

Business owners.

Creators.

Many build entire lives around overcompensation.

Their calendars become overloaded.

Their nervous systems become overwhelmed.

Their identities become tied to productivity.

And eventually, urgency stops feeling like a state they enter.

It becomes the only place they know how to live.

The Exhausted Professional

One of the least discussed experiences of ADHD is professional masking.

Many highly intelligent adults with ADHD become skilled at compensating for executive dysfunction.

Multiple calendars.

Obsessive reminders.

Hyperorganization systems.

Late-night catch-up sessions.

Working twice as hard just to appear "normal."

The outside world often mistakes this for ambition.

But internally, many professionals are barely holding themselves together.

They fear:

- forgetting something important
- disappointing people
- being exposed as disorganized
- losing control
- failing publicly

That fear creates chronic hypervigilance.

And chronic hypervigilance keeps the nervous system activated.

Many high-functioning adults with ADHD are never truly resting.

Even when their bodies are still, their minds continue:

- planning
- replaying
- worrying
- scanning

- anticipating
- overthinking

Over time, that constant activation becomes physical.

Headaches.

Burnout.

Insomnia.

Panic attacks.

Emotional numbness.

Irritability.

Depression.

Substance use.

Exhaustion.

And yet, many continue to function on the outside for years before the collapse becomes visible.

◈

Success and Silent Collapse

One of the most dangerous aspects of high-functioning ADHD is that people often do not recognize the suffering until the collapse becomes visible.

The person is still working.

Still producing.

Still succeeding.

Still showing up.

So outsiders assume everything is fine.

But inside, the nervous system may already be close to shutting down.

Many people with ADHD survive on adrenaline.

Deadlines.

Pressure.

Urgency.

Overcommitment.

The problem is that adrenaline is not sustainable.

Eventually, the nervous system crashes.

Burnout is extremely common among high-functioning adults with ADHD, especially those who have spent years overcompensating for executive dysfunction through perfectionism and overwork.

Many become addicted to productivity itself.

Not because they love working.

Because slowing down forces them to feel everything they have spent years outrunning.

The exhaustion.

The anxiety.

The overstimulation.

The emotional pain.

The fear of inadequacy.

Work becomes regulation.

Achievement becomes dopamine.

And eventually, rest begins to feel unsafe.

◈

High-Functioning Women and Invisible ADHD

Historically, ADHD research focused heavily on hyperactive boys.

As a result, countless women remained undiagnosed for years, sometimes even decades.

Many women with ADHD learned early how to mask their symptoms socially.

They became:

- outwardly organized
- emotionally accommodating
- hyperaware of social expectations
- perfectionistic
- people-pleasing
- self-critical

But underneath that adaptation often lived:

- anxiety
- emotional exhaustion
- chronic overwhelm
- shame
- sensory overload
- nervous system fatigue
- rejection sensitivity

Many high-functioning women with ADHD become masters at appearing capable while privately drowning.

Researchers and authors such as Sari Solden helped bring attention to the emotional lives of women with ADHD, particularly the hidden burden of masking, shame, and chronic self-doubt.

Many women were not disruptive enough to attract attention in school.

So instead of being recognized as neurologically overwhelmed, they were labeled:

- emotional
- anxious
- dramatic
- disorganized
- lazy
- too sensitive

That misunderstanding created enormous emotional damage.

Especially because many women internalized those struggles privately for years before receiving a diagnosis or validation.

Some women do not discover they have ADHD until adulthood.

Sometimes after:

- burnout
- relationship struggles
- parenting challenges
- anxiety disorders
- depression
- addiction
- chronic overwhelm

And suddenly, their entire life begins to make sense through a different lens.

Not moral failure.

Neurological dysregulation.

That realization can be both heartbreaking and liberating.

◈

High-Functioning Men and Emotional Suppression

Many men with ADHD experience a different form of invisibility.

From an early age, many boys are taught to:

- stop crying
- calm down
- toughen up
- stop overreacting
- stop being emotional

But emotional dysregulation is often deeply connected to ADHD.

So instead of learning emotional regulation, many boys learn emotional suppression.

Over time, that suppression can become:

- anger
- emotional shutdown
- work addiction
- impulsivity
- substance use
- avoidance
- relationship conflict
- emotional numbness

Many high-functioning men with ADHD are praised for overworking while privately collapsing under the pressure.

Society often rewards:

- hustle
- overcommitment
- productivity

- emotional suppression

But nervous systems do not care about social praise.

Eventually, the body begins collecting the cost.

Burnout.

Insomnia.

Hypertension.

Addiction.

Depression.

Emotional isolation.

Many men spend decades believing they are simply "bad at emotions," when in reality, they were never taught nervous system regulation.

That misunderstanding damages countless relationships and lives.

◈

Perfectionism as Survival

Many people do not realize how deeply perfectionism is connected to shame.

Especially ADHD shame.

When children are repeatedly met with criticism, correction, disappointment, or negative feedback, many begin using perfectionism as protection. It becomes a way to feel safer in a world that often makes them feel inadequate.

If they can just:

- work harder
- perform better
- avoid mistakes
- overprepare
- Overachieve

Maybe they can finally avoid rejection.

Maybe they can finally stop feeling like a problem.

But perfectionism becomes exhausting.

It is exhaustion disguised as discipline.

And for many people with ADHD, perfectionism creates a brutal cycle.

The person becomes intensely afraid of failure.

That fear creates overwhelm.

Overwhelm leads to procrastination.

Procrastination creates shame.

Shame turns into panic.

Panic creates urgency.

Urgency finally forces action.

Then exhaustion follows.

Again and again.

Many high-functioning adults with ADHD live inside this cycle for years.

Sometimes for entire careers.

And because society often rewards achievement while ignoring nervous system health, people continue applauding the very behaviors that are quietly destroying them internally.

◈

The Fear of Falling Behind

Many individuals with ADHD quietly carry a lifelong fear that, one day, people will discover they are not functioning as well as they appear.

That fear fuels:

- overworking
- masking

- hyper-independence
- people-pleasing
- emotional suppression
- perfectionism

Many become terrified of slowing down because slowing down feels emotionally dangerous.

Silence feels dangerous.

Rest feels dangerous.

Stillness feels dangerous.

Because underneath the constant movement, there are often years of:

- shame
- emotional pain
- overstimulation
- fear of inadequacy
- rejection sensitivity
- nervous system exhaustion

This is why many high-functioning adults with ADHD struggle so profoundly with self-worth.

Their worth became tied to performance.

Not humanity.

Productivity became identity.

Achievement became emotional safety.

And eventually, they stopped knowing who they were outside of functioning. They learned how to keep going.

◈

Why High Achievers Break Quietly

Some of the most misunderstood individuals with ADHD are the ones who appear successful on the outside.

Because people often assume:

- achievement means wellness
- intelligence means regulation
- success means emotional stability

None of those assumptions are true.

Many high-achieving adults with ADHD are:

- chronically overstimulated
- emotionally dysregulated
- sleep-deprived
- constantly masking
- terrified of disappointing people
- deeply burned out

And because they continue to function externally, they are often the last to receive help.

Sometimes help only comes after:

- panic attacks
- addiction
- nervous breakdowns
- emotional collapse
- damaged relationships
- severe burnout

That is why understanding high-functioning ADHD matters so deeply.

Because many people who are suffering the most are also the ones who appear the strongest.

And often, the strongest-looking people are simply the ones who became the best at hiding their exhaustion.

That is the hidden reality of high-functioning ADHD.

Gifted.

Capable.

Creative.

Brilliant.

Driven.

And completely exhausted beneath the performance.

Not because they are weak.

Because they have spent their entire lives surviving inside nervous systems that never truly learned how to rest.

CHAPTER FOUR

The Nervous System Nobody Could See

For decades, ADHD was misunderstood as a simple behavioral problem.

A focus problem.

A classroom problem.

A discipline problem.

Children moved too much.

Talked too much.

Interrupted too much.

Couldn't sit still long enough.

Couldn't pay attention long enough.

Could not seem to "control themselves."

But that oversimplified narrative damaged millions of people.

Because beneath the visible behaviors was something far more complex: a dysregulated nervous system.

When people fail to understand the nervous system beneath behavior, they often mistake survival responses for personality flaws.

That misunderstanding changes lives.

Children begin believing they are:

- lazy
- dramatic

- difficult
- too emotional
- irresponsible
- broken

When in reality, many are neurologically overwhelmed.

Modern ADHD research is beginning to reflect what countless individuals have privately experienced for most of their lives:

ADHD is not simply about attention.

It is deeply connected to:

- emotional regulation
- executive functioning
- dopamine regulation
- stress response systems
- nervous system activation
- trauma overlap
- sensory processing
- rejection sensitivity
- emotional overwhelm

And once people truly understand the nervous system beneath ADHD, the entire condition begins to look different.

Not smaller.

Not simpler.

Far larger than the old narrative allowed.

◈

ADHD Is More Than Attention

One of the greatest failures in public understanding of ADHD may be the name itself:

Attention Deficit Hyperactivity Disorder.

The label leads many people to imagine only the most visible traits:

- distractibility
- hyperactivity
- restlessness
- impulsivity

But ADHD extends far beyond simple attention problems.

Many clinicians and researchers now recognize ADHD as a condition deeply connected to executive functioning and self-regulation. Researchers such as Russell A. Barkley have repeatedly emphasized that ADHD involves impairments in the systems responsible for regulating behavior, emotion, attention, and action over time.

That distinction changes everything.

Because executive functioning affects:

- emotional regulation
- planning
- working memory
- task initiation
- organization
- time perception
- impulse control
- self-monitoring
- emotional inhibition

In other words, ADHD affects far more than attention.

It affects how individuals manage themselves from the inside.

And when self-regulation is impaired, nearly every part of life can become harder.

School.

Relationships.

Work.

Parenting.

Addiction recovery.

Finances.

Sleep.

Stress tolerance.

Emotional resilience.

ADHD follows people into every part of life because the nervous system follows them there.

That is what many outsiders fail to understand.

ADHD is not something a person can simply "turn off."

Many people with ADHD spend their entire lives trying to regulate nervous systems that feel overstimulated, emotionally activated, under-rewarded, or overwhelmed.

That effort becomes exhausting.

Over time, that exhaustion becomes cumulative.

And cumulative nervous system exhaustion can change the way people see themselves, relate to others, and move through the world.

◈

The Emotional Brain

For many years, emotional dysregulation was not widely considered a core part of ADHD.

Today, that understanding is changing.

Many clinicians now recognize emotional dysregulation as one of the most impairing and painful aspects of ADHD.

It can include:

- rapid mood shifts
- emotional flooding
- impulsive reactions
- frustration intolerance

- irritability
- emotional overwhelm
- rejection sensitivity
- shame spirals
- emotional rumination

Many individuals with ADHD do not simply "feel emotions strongly."

They often experience emotions quickly, intensely, and with limited time to regulate before the reaction takes over.

That distinction matters.

The ADHD nervous system often struggles with emotional braking systems.

Emotions can arrive quickly.

Powerfully.

Overwhelmingly.

And by the time the person consciously recognizes what is happening, the nervous system may already be fully activated.

This creates enormous misunderstandings in relationships.

Especially because many emotional reactions happen so fast that individuals themselves may struggle to explain them afterward.

They may later say:

- "I overreacted."
- "I don't know why I got so emotional."
- "I knew I was escalating, but I couldn't stop."
- "Everything suddenly felt overwhelming."

That is not simply immaturity.

In many cases, it reflects nervous system dysregulation.

Researchers including Thomas E. Brown and Edward M. Hallowell have increasingly highlighted emotional regulation difficulties as central ADHD experiences rather than secondary side effects.

That shift in understanding is critical.

Because for generations, many individuals with ADHD were punished for emotional dysregulation instead of being taught emotional regulation.

Those are not the same thing.

Punishment creates shame.

Regulation creates healing.

◈

The Nervous System in Survival Mode

One of the most important contributions of modern neuroscience is the way it has clarified the relationship between chronic stress, nervous system activation, and psychological functioning.

Researchers such as Bessel van der Kolk, author of *The Body Keeps the Score*, have extensively explored how trauma can affect nervous system regulation.

That connection becomes especially important when discussing ADHD.

Because many individuals with ADHD grow up inside chronic nervous system stress.

Not always because of catastrophic trauma.

Sometimes because of repeated emotional overwhelm.

Repeated correction.

Repeated shame.

Repeated criticism.

Repeated experiences of failure.

Repeated rejection.

Repeated dysregulation.

Over time, the nervous system begins to adapt around survival.

The child becomes hyperaware.

Hypervigilant.

Emotionally reactive.

Sensitive to criticism.

Sensitive to changes in tone.

Sensitive to rejection.

Many individuals with ADHD become experts at scanning their environments emotionally.

Watching faces.

Monitoring reactions.

Trying to determine whether someone is upset with them.

That hyperawareness can later resemble:

- anxiety disorders
- trauma responses
- emotional hypervigilance
- rejection sensitivity
- attachment insecurity

And sometimes, those conditions genuinely coexist.

That overlap is one reason ADHD is so often clinically misunderstood.

Because ADHD rarely exists in isolation.

It frequently overlaps with:

- anxiety
- depression
- trauma
- substance use disorders
- sleep disorders
- sensory processing difficulties
- mood dysregulation

- learning disorders
- attachment disturbances

The nervous system becomes layered.

Complex.

Multidimensional.

And many individuals spend years being treated for symptoms without anyone recognizing the underlying ADHD-related nervous system dysregulation beneath them.

◈

When Trauma and ADHD Collide

One of the most complicated conversations in modern mental health involves the overlap between trauma and ADHD.

This discussion requires nuance.

Because trauma can mimic ADHD symptoms.

And ADHD can increase a person's vulnerability to traumatic experiences.

That overlap is clinically significant.

Trauma can affect:

- concentration
- impulse control
- emotional regulation
- sleep
- attention
- executive functioning
- nervous system activation

This means trauma responses can sometimes resemble ADHD presentations.

At the same time, individuals with ADHD may experience:

- more academic struggles

- more social rejection
- more impulsive risk-taking
- more emotional dysregulation
- more interpersonal conflict
- more negative feedback
- increased vulnerability to addiction

Over time, these experiences can create additional emotional wounds.

This is why many clinicians now approach ADHD through a trauma-informed lens.

Not because ADHD is caused solely by trauma.

But because nervous system dysregulation and life experiences often interact in powerful ways.

Gabor Maté discusses this extensively in *Scattered Minds,* emphasizing the role early emotional environments may play in shaping attention regulation, stress systems, and emotional development.

Not all ADHD experts fully agree on causation models, and that distinction matters. Still, the broader conversation surrounding emotional environments, stress, attachment, and nervous system development has become increasingly important in modern ADHD discussions.

What matters most clinically is this:

Many individuals with ADHD are carrying neurodevelopmental dysregulation and emotional wounds at the same time.

And treatment becomes far more effective when both realities are acknowledged.

◈

The Overstimulated Brain

Many individuals with ADHD spend their lives inside nervous systems overloaded by stimulation.

That overstimulation may come from many directions:

- sensory overload
- emotional overload
- cognitive overload
- social overload
- technological overload

The modern world intensifies all of it.

Notifications.

Social media.

Constant accessibility.

Noise.

Pressure.

Urgency.

Information overload.

The ADHD brain often struggles to filter incoming stimulation efficiently.

Everything competes for attention at once.

And when the nervous system cannot prioritize effectively, overwhelm builds quickly.

That overwhelm may appear externally as:

- irritability
- avoidance
- shutdown
- impulsivity
- emotional flooding

- distraction
- exhaustion

Children often experience this in classrooms.

Adults experience it in workplaces, relationships, parenting, and modern digital environments.

The problem is that many people interpret overstimulation morally rather than neurologically.

They see:

- laziness
- disorganization
- emotional instability
- irresponsibility

Instead of recognizing nervous system overload.

That misunderstanding can profoundly damage self-esteem.

Especially because many individuals with ADHD are highly self-aware.

They know they are struggling.

They simply cannot regulate themselves consistently.

And that inconsistency becomes emotionally painful.

◈

The Invisible Weight of Shame

Shame may be one of the most psychologically destructive experiences associated with ADHD.

Not because ADHD automatically creates shame.

But because misunderstanding creates shame.

Repeated correction creates shame.

Repeated failure creates shame.

Repeated rejection creates shame.

Over time, many individuals begin to internalize deeply painful beliefs:

- I'm lazy.
- I'm too emotional.
- I'm too much.
- I ruin things.
- I disappoint people.
- I can't get my life together.
- Something is wrong with me.

Those beliefs become emotionally embedded.

And eventually, many adults with ADHD stop seeing dysregulation as something they experience.

They begin seeing it as who they are.

That identity wound can be devastating.

Especially among high-functioning individuals.

Because many become successful on the outside while privately feeling defective on the inside.

That contradiction creates profound loneliness.

The outside world praises their achievement.

Meanwhile, the person privately feels:

- overwhelmed
- emotionally exhausted
- chronically anxious
- fraudulent
- ashamed
- overstimulated

Many individuals spend years believing they are failing at adulthood when they are actually surviving inside chronically dysregulated nervous systems.

And when they finally understand that difference, the realization can change everything.

◈

The Rejection-Sensitive Nervous System

One of the least understood aspects of ADHD involves rejection sensitivity.

Many individuals with ADHD experience criticism, disappointment, exclusion, or perceived rejection with extraordinary emotional intensity.

This experience is often referred to as Rejection Sensitivity Dysphoria, or RSD.

Although RSD is still being studied formally, countless individuals with ADHD describe:

- overwhelming emotional distress after criticism
- intense fear of disappointing others
- emotional spirals after perceived rejection
- people-pleasing
- emotional masking
- conflict avoidance
- shame attacks
- emotional rumination

For many individuals, rejection does not feel mild.

It feels catastrophic.

Neurologically overwhelming.

Emotionally consuming.

And often, the intensity arrives before the person has time to understand what is happening.

This becomes especially painful in relationships.

Many individuals with ADHD become hyperaware of:

- changes in tone
- body language
- emotional distance
- shifts in conflict
- subtle criticism
- delayed replies
- facial expressions

They are not simply "overthinking."

In many cases, their nervous system is scanning for emotional danger.

Because years of correction, criticism, misunderstanding, or rejection can train the body to anticipate pain before it arrives.

That kind of hypervigilance is exhausting.

Unfortunately, many people only see the reaction from the outside.

They see someone who seems too sensitive.

Too dramatic.

Too emotional.

Too intense.

But emotional intensity is not weakness.

It is nervous system activation.

And that distinction matters enormously.

◈

The Addiction Connection

One of the most painful realities surrounding ADHD is its connection to addiction vulnerability.

Research has consistently shown higher rates of substance use disorders among individuals with ADHD, but this overlap is not simply a matter of poor choices or weak willpower.

For many individuals, it begins with a search for regulation.

Relief from:

- emotional flooding
- racing thoughts
- overstimulation
- anxiety
- nervous system exhaustion
- internal chaos

When the nervous system feels constantly dysregulated, anything that offers temporary relief can become powerful.

For some, substances may seem to provide what their nervous system has been trying to find for years:

- slowing
- stimulation
- focus
- emotional escape
- numbness
- relief

That relief may be temporary, but the nervous system remembers it.

And what provides relief can quickly become reinforcing.

Researchers including Gabor Maté have discussed addiction as deeply connected to emotional pain, unmet needs, and attempts to regulate dysregulated nervous systems.

For many individuals with ADHD, substances may initially feel less like intoxication and more like temporary access to calm.

Temporary access to quiet.

Temporary access to control.

That does not remove accountability.

But it does change understanding.

And understanding changes treatment.

Because when addiction is treated only as a behavior problem, the deeper nervous system struggle is often missed. That is how many people remain trapped in cycles of relapse, shame, and emotional exhaustion.

◈

The Future of ADHD Research

Modern ADHD research is evolving rapidly.

And perhaps the most hopeful part of that evolution is this:

the conversation is finally becoming more human.

For decades, ADHD discussions focused heavily on behavior control.

Now, the field is increasingly recognizing the deeper systems involved:

- emotional regulation
- trauma overlap
- nervous system functioning
- executive dysfunction
- rejection sensitivity
- sensory processing
- burnout
- masking
- emotional exhaustion

Researchers are also exploring:

- neuroplasticity
- emotional regulation therapies
- mindfulness-based interventions
- nervous system regulation

- digital overstimulation
- trauma-informed ADHD treatment
- exercise and dopamine regulation
- sleep and executive functioning
- psychedelic-assisted mental health research
- ADHD in women and underserved populations

The field is changing.

Slowly.

But meaningfully.

And perhaps most importantly, people with ADHD are beginning to tell their own stories more openly.

Not only clinicians.

Not only researchers.

But the people living inside these nervous systems every single day.

That matters.

Because lived experience and scientific understanding should never compete.

They should inform each other.

The strongest understanding comes when both are respected together.

◈

What the World Missed

For years, society misunderstood ADHD because it focused too heavily on visible behavior and not enough on invisible suffering.

People saw:

- distraction
- impulsivity

- hyperactivity
- emotional intensity

But they missed:

- shame
- exhaustion
- overstimulation
- hypervigilance
- nervous system dysregulation
- emotional pain
- rejection sensitivity
- chronic self-criticism

And perhaps that is one of the greatest tragedies surrounding ADHD.

So many individuals spent years believing they were broken.

When in reality, many were carrying overwhelmed nervous systems they had never been taught how to understand, support, or regulate.

That realization can change lives.

Because once people stop seeing themselves as defective, they can begin seeing themselves more truthfully:

not weak.

Not lazy.

Not broken.

But neurologically overwhelmed human beings trying to survive inside electric minds that have been working too hard for too long.

CHAPTER FIVE

Hyperfocus

Most people think ADHD means an inability to focus.

That misunderstanding has shaped decades of stigma, shame, oversimplified diagnoses, and public confusion.

Because many people with ADHD do not suffer from a lack of focus.

They struggle with inconsistent control over focus.

And sometimes, when stimulation, emotional intensity, urgency, novelty, creativity, curiosity, or dopamine align in exactly the right way, the ADHD brain does something extraordinary.

It locks in.

Completely.

Hours disappear.

The outside world fades.

Hunger disappears.

Fatigue disappears.

Time disappears.

Sometimes, even relationships begin to disappear.

The person becomes consumed.

Absorbed.

Electrically connected to whatever has captured the nervous system.

This phenomenon is commonly referred to as hyperfocus.

And for many people with ADHD, hyperfocus becomes both:

- one of their greatest strengths
- one of the most psychologically dangerous experiences they can have

Because hyperfocus is not simply concentration.

It is absorption.

Total neurological immersion.

And once people understand hyperfocus, they begin to understand why so many individuals with ADHD become:

- innovators
- artists
- entrepreneurs
- musicians
- clinicians
- writers
- coders
- creators
- performers
- visionaries

The same nervous system that struggles to regulate attention can sometimes channel extraordinary focus when it is emotionally activated.

That paradox confuses people.

Especially those who only understand ADHD through stereotypes.

Because the same person who forgets bills, loses keys, misses appointments, and struggles through school may also possess the ability to:

- research obsessively for twelve hours straight
- create extraordinary art overnight

- build businesses from nothing
- become consumed by innovation
- master highly stimulating subjects rapidly
- connect to ideas with extraordinary emotional intensity

That contradiction is ADHD.

And for many people, it becomes both beautiful and destructive at the same time.

◈

The Obsession Loop

Many people with ADHD do not simply "like" things.

They become consumed by them.

An idea enters the mind, and suddenly, the nervous system lights up.

Research begins.

Videos begin.

Books begin.

Planning begins.

Thinking begins.

Dreaming begins.

The brain becomes electrically attached to possibility.

And when that happens, the outside world often fades emotionally.

Many people with ADHD describe hyperfocus as almost entering another psychological dimension.

Time stops functioning normally.

Three hours can feel like twenty minutes.

An entire night can disappear.

The person forgets:

- to eat
- to sleep

- to respond to messages
- to rest
- to slow down

Because the nervous system is finally receiving what it has been searching for: stimulation powerful enough to fully activate it.

This is one reason ADHD can appear contradictory from the outside.

The same person who struggles profoundly with routine tasks may become almost unstoppable when emotionally connected to something meaningful.

Researchers such as Edward M. Hallowell and John J. Ratey have discussed this paradox extensively in works such as *Driven to Distraction* and *Delivered from Distraction.*

Hyperfocus demonstrates that ADHD is not simply a deficit of attention.

It is often a dysregulation of attention allocation.

The brain struggles not only with sustaining attention, but also with disengaging attention once fully activated.

That distinction matters enormously.

Because many people with ADHD are not "lazy."

Their nervous systems simply require different levels of stimulation and emotional engagement to activate consistently.

◈

When Time Disappears

One of the defining features of hyperfocus is distorted time perception.

Minutes disappear.

Hours disappear.

Sometimes, entire days seem to vanish.

Many people with ADHD experience profound "time blindness," meaning the nervous system struggles to perceive and regulate time accurately and consistently.

This becomes especially risky during hyperfocus.

The person may intend to work for:

- thirty minutes
- one hour
- a short period

Then suddenly realize:

- it is 3:00 a.m.
- they forgot to eat
- they missed obligations
- they ignored messages
- they skipped responsibilities
- their body is exhausted

But internally, the nervous system still feels activated.

Still engaged.

Still searching.

This creates enormous tension in adulthood.

Because hyperfocus can produce:

- brilliance
- innovation
- productivity
- creativity

while also creating:

- neglect
- imbalance
- exhaustion
- relationship strain

- burnout
- physical depletion

That is why hyperfocus cannot simply be romanticized as a "gift."

It must be understood honestly.

Because many people with ADHD quietly harm themselves through obsession.

◈

Three in the Morning

Many people with ADHD know this feeling intimately.

The house is dark.

Everyone else is asleep.

But the mind is fully awake.

Ideas begin to explode. Research tabs multiply. Projects expand. Thoughts accelerate.

For the first time all day, the nervous system may finally feel stimulated, engaged, and emotionally alive.

For many people with ADHD, nighttime can become psychologically risky because external stimulation decreases while internal stimulation increases. The world becomes quiet, but the mind becomes louder.

Silence creates space for:

- Ideas
- Rumination
- Obsession
- Planning
- emotional replay
- Creativity
- Anxiety.

This is why many individuals with ADHD feel most mentally alive at night. Their thoughts feel sharper. Their energy returns. Their imagination opens. Their focus suddenly becomes available.

And while hyperfocus can create extraordinary productivity, it can also disrupt nervous system balance at the same time.

Sleep becomes sacrificed.

Recovery becomes sacrificed.

The body becomes sacrificed.

Eventually, many individuals begin living inside chronic exhaustion while continuing to function on dopamine, urgency, and adrenaline alone.

Neurologically, this lifestyle becomes unsustainable.

Unfortunately, society often rewards it temporarily, especially among:

- entrepreneurs
- creatives
- executives
- clinicians
- performers
- students
- innovators

People applaud the results while ignoring the nervous system cost underneath them.

◈

The Productivity High

One of the least discussed aspects of hyperfocus is how emotionally addictive productivity can become for people with ADHD, especially high-functioning adults.

Many adults with ADHD spend years learning that achievement can temporarily quiet shame. Success can temporarily quiet self-doubt. Productivity can temporarily create dopamine.

And once achievement becomes emotionally regulating, people may begin chasing it compulsively.

This creates a form of productivity addiction.

Not because the person simply "loves success," but because productivity becomes neurological relief.

For a moment, the individual finally feels:

- focused
- valuable
- competent
- emotionally engaged
- mentally activated

That feeling can become intoxicating, especially for people who have spent years feeling disorganized, misunderstood, inconsistent, and emotionally overwhelmed.

Achievement becomes proof that they are not broken.

But eventually, the nervous system pays for it.

Hyperfocus often ignores biological limits.

The body still need:

- sleep
- rest
- nutrition
- emotional recovery
- nervous system decompression

Hyperfocus frequently overrides all of them.

And eventually, the individual crashes.

Burnout becomes inevitable when obsession replaces regulation.

◈

The Cost of Genius

Society romanticizes obsession, especially when obsession produces results.

The artist who never sleeps.

The entrepreneur working nonstop.

The creator consumed by vision.

The clinician giving everything away emotionally.

The student surviving on caffeine and panic.

The executive running entirely on urgency.

Modern culture often praises nervous system self-destruction when it leads to achievement.

But nervous systems are not machines.

Many people with ADHD spend years believing:

- exhaustion equals dedication
- overworking equals worth
- productivity equals value
- and rest equals weakness

That belief can become psychologically devastating, especially for individuals who already struggle deeply with self-worth.

So hyperfocus becomes more than concentration.

It becomes identity.

And when identity becomes attached entirely to output, slowing down can feel terrifying. Rest no longer feels safe. Pausing feels like failure. The absence of productivity begins to feel like the absence of value.

The individual may fear:

- failure
- irrelevance
- rejection

- Disappointment
- worthlessness

That fear can drive many high-functioning adults with ADHD far beyond healthy nervous system limits.

Eventually:

- anxiety increases
- irritability rises
- emotional dysregulation worsens
- relationships deteriorate
- burnout deepens
- sleep collapses
- substances may become tempting
- nervous system exhaustion becomes chronic

The same mind capable of brilliance begins turning against itself neurologically.

◈

The Relationship Casualties

Hyperfocus can affect relationships profoundly, especially romantic relationships.

Many people with ADHD can hyperfocus emotionally on people in the same way they hyperfocus on interests. In the early stages, relationships can feel intoxicating.

The person may become:

- emotionally consumed
- intensely attentive
- deeply connected
- highly affectionate
- constantly engaged

The nervous system floods with dopamine.

But over time, as novelty decreases, attention regulation difficulties may reappear.

Not because love disappeared.

Because dopamine regulation shifted.

That transition can create enormous misunderstanding in relationships. Partners may feel:

- ignored
- emotionally abandoned
- forgotten
- deprioritized
- Meanwhile, the person with ADHD may feel:
- ashamed
- confused
- overwhelmed
- emotionally flooded

This is why understanding ADHD neurologically becomes so important in relationships.

Many conflicts are not caused by a lack of caring. They are caused by dysregulation.

At the same time, hyperfocus can also create unhealthy relationship intensity. Many individuals with ADHD may:

- attach quickly
- idealize deeply
- emotionally merge rapidly
- fear abandonment intensely
- overinvest emotionally

This may be especially true for individuals with:

- trauma overlap
- rejection sensitivity

- attachment wounds

That emotional intensity can be beautiful.

It can also become destabilizing.

◈

The Hyperfocus Child

Children with ADHD often experience hyperfocus long before anyone has a name for it.

Parents may notice that the child:

- becomes intensely absorbed in specific interests
- researches endlessly
- memorizes details rapidly
- loses track of time
- ignores their surroundings completely when engaged

This can create confusion.

How can a child struggle to focus in school, yet spend six straight hours consumed by:

- LEGO bricks
- gaming
- drawing
- dinosaurs
- music
- sports statistics
- computers
- art
- storytelling

The answer is not laziness.

The answer is stimulation.

Emotionally meaningful stimulation can dramatically change nervous system activation. Interest, novelty, challenge, and emotional connection can make attention suddenly available.

That does not mean the child is choosing to fail elsewhere. It means their nervous system responds differently depending on dopamine engagement.

This distinction is critical in education.

Many children with ADHD are punished for executive dysfunction while their extraordinary capacities remain misunderstood. Their difficulty with attention is often mistaken for defiance, carelessness, or lack of effort.

Some children are not disengaged from learning.

They are disengaged from environments that fail to activate them emotionally.

That misunderstanding can shape an entire academic life.

◈

The Creative Explosion

Many of the world's most innovative minds may have carried nervous systems that would resemble ADHD presentations today.

Creativity and ADHD frequently overlap because ADHD minds often excel at:

- divergent thinking
- rapid association
- novelty generation
- emotional intuition
- pattern recognition
- imaginative problem-solving

The ADHD mind often sees connections other people miss.

Not because it is "better."

Because it processes information differently.

Rapidly.

Associatively.

Emotionally.

This difference can create extraordinary creative potential.

But without regulation, creativity can also become emotionally costly.

Many creatives with ADHD experience:

- emotional volatility
- burnout
- inconsistency
- obsession cycles
- depression after projects end
- identity collapse when not creating

Creation itself can become neurological stimulation.

The brain begins to depend on emotional intensity to feel alive.

Over time, that dependency becomes exhausting.

◈

When Hyperfocus Turns Dark

Hyperfocus is not always productive.

That matters.

The same mechanism that creates brilliance can also intensify suffering.

Many individuals hyperfocus on:

- anxiety
- shame
- rejection
- conflict
- traumatic memories

- emotional pain
- addiction
- unhealthy relationships
- obsessive thoughts

The nervous system locks onto emotionally charged material. Once activated, disengaging can become difficult.

This is why ADHD frequently overlaps with:

- rumination
- anxiety disorders
- obsessive thinking
- emotional spirals

The mind does not simply think.

It loops.

And when that loop attaches itself to shame or fear, the nervous system can remain caught in emotional overwhelm for hours, sometimes even days.

Many individuals describe:

- replaying conversations endlessly
- obsessing over mistakes
- catastrophizing rejection
- emotionally spiraling after criticism

That is hyperfocus too.

Not productive hyperfocus.

Painful hyperfocus.

◈

Burning Through the Brain

Many high-functioning adults with ADHD unknowingly spend years burning through their nervous systems.

Running on:

- caffeine
- adrenaline
- urgency
- obsession
- pressure
- dopamine-seeking

The body adapts for a while.

But eventually:

- sleep suffers
- cortisol rises
- emotional regulation worsens
- anxiety intensifies
- exhaustion deepens
- burnout becomes chronic

This is one reason ADHD treatment cannot focus only on productivity.

Many individuals are already productive.

The deeper issue is sustainability.

The nervous system must eventually learn:

- pacing
- regulation
- boundaries
- rest tolerance
- emotional awareness
- nervous system recovery

Without those skills, hyperfocus can become self-destruction disguised as ambition.

◈

Harnessing Hyperfocus Without Self-Destruction

Hyperfocus itself is not the enemy.

Unregulated hyperfocus is.

When understood and supported properly, hyperfocus can become extraordinary.

Many people with ADHD accomplish incredible things because of their ability to:

- emotionally immerse
- innovate deeply
- create intensely
- learn rapidly
- connect passionately
- think divergently

The goal is not to eliminate intensity.

The goal is to regulate it.

This means learning:

- when to engage deeply
- when to pause
- when to rest
- when to disconnect
- when to protect the nervous system

That balance can be life-changing.

Especially for people with ADHD who have spent years believing their intensity itself was the problem.

It is not.

The absence of regulation is the problem.

The electric mind is capable of:

- brilliance
- innovation

- empathy
- vision
- creativity
- transformation

But electricity without grounding eventually burns through everything it touches.

That is the paradox of hyperfocus.

It can build extraordinary lives.

It can also silently destroy exhausted nervous systems beneath achievement.

For many people with ADHD, learning the difference becomes one of the most important journeys of their lives.

CHAPTER SIX

Brains Built for Fire

Some minds are built for rhythm.

Others are built for ignition.

They do not move quietly through ordinary emotional bandwidth. They feel life with unusual force. They think quickly, imagine deeply, dream boldly, love intensely, obsess fully, and create endlessly.

Many ADHD minds are not wired for emotional neutrality.

They are wired for fire.

That fire often appears early in childhood.

The child who asks endless questions.

The child who dismantles objects just to understand how they work.

The child who cannot stop imagining.

The child who feels almost physically overwhelmed by boredom.

The child who keeps creating stories, drawings, inventions, fantasies, plans, and possibilities before anyone has taught them what to do with that intensity.

Many children with ADHD are not disconnected from the world.

They are overconnected to it.

Life enters the nervous system at full volume.

Sounds.

Ideas.

Emotions.

Patterns.

Conflict.

Curiosity.

Possibility.

And when the nervous system absorbs life this intensely, many people with ADHD spend years feeling like they are "too much" for the environments around them.

Too loud.

Too emotional.

Too energetic.

Too intense.

Too imaginative.

Too impulsive.

But what if that intensity was never only pathology?

What if some of it was untamed potential inside nervous systems that were never taught how to regulate their own fire?

That possibility changes the conversation around ADHD.

Because throughout history, some of the people who changed the world may have carried nervous systems that would strongly resemble ADHD presentations today.

Visionaries.

Artists.

Inventors.

Entrepreneurs.

Revolutionaries.

People who refused to think conventionally because their minds could not stay confined inside conventional thinking.

The electric mind often refuses to remain emotionally asleep.

And while that fire can become destructive without regulation, it can also become extraordinary.

◈

The Child Who Couldn't Stay Inside the Lines

Many people with ADHD grow up hearing different versions of the same message:

"Calm down."

"Slow down."

"Focus."

"Sit still."

"Pay attention."

"Why are you acting like this?"

Over time, those corrections do more than guide behavior.

Many children begin to internalize the belief that their natural nervous system is wrong.

That wound can become deep, especially because many children with ADHD are not trying to create problems.

They are trying to survive stimulation.

The classroom feels too loud.

The lights feel too bright.

The boredom feels unbearable.

The emotions feel too large to hold.

The nervous system feels electrically alive, with nowhere safe to place the energy.

And yet, even while struggling in traditional environments, many children with ADHD demonstrate extraordinary abilities:

- creativity
- emotional depth
- imagination
- innovation
- humor
- intuition

- rapid learning under stimulation
- unusual pattern recognition

The problem is that many educational systems reward:

- repetition
- passive attention
- stillness
- conformity
- standardized pacing

But many ADHD minds were never built for passive engagement.

They were built for activation.

That mismatch creates emotional pain early.

Many children with ADHD begin to sense, long before they have the language for it, that they are different.

They feel it in the frustration.

In the overstimulation.

In the shame.

In the emotional intensity.

In the exhausting effort to regulate themselves again and again.

Eventually, many begin hiding parts of themselves just to survive socially.

That is where masking begins.

◈

The Masking of Brilliance

One of the most psychologically exhausting experiences associated with ADHD is masking intelligence inside dysregulation.

Or masking dysregulation beneath intelligence.

Many gifted people with ADHD become skilled at appearing functional on the outside while privately battling:

- overwhelm
- emotional flooding
- anxiety
- exhaustion
- chaos
- disorganization
- burnout

This becomes especially common among high-functioning adults.

The world sees:

- charisma
- creativity
- productivity
- leadership
- achievement

But privately, the nervous system may be collapsing beneath the performance.

Many people with ADHD become extraordinary at surviving through:

- adrenaline
- urgency
- pressure
- hyperfocus
- overworking
- perfectionism

Society often rewards these behaviors, especially in high-performance environments.

But the nervous system always collects the bill eventually.

Burnout becomes inevitable when a person lives too long in chronic activation.

And yet, many people with ADHD continue pushing themselves beyond healthy limits because the world keeps applauding the very behaviors that are quietly destroying them internally.

The entrepreneur working eighteen hours straight.

The clinician emotionally overextending for everyone else.

The executive surviving entirely on caffeine and urgency.

The creator who cannot stop producing because stillness feels emotionally dangerous.

The world often labels these individuals "driven."

But many are not driven by peace.

Many are driven by nervous system survival.

That distinction matters enormously.

◈

Why ADHD Minds Often Become Visionary

Many ADHD minds think associatively rather than linearly.

The brain constantly connects:

- ideas
- emotions
- possibilities
- patterns
- concepts
- visions

This creates enormous internal stimulation.

It can also create extraordinary innovation.

Researchers such as Ned Hallowell and John J. Ratey have extensively discussed about how ADHD minds often demonstrate strong divergent thinking capacities.

Divergent thinking allows individuals to rapidly generate:

- possibilities
- solutions
- interpretations
- creative alternatives

Many people with ADHD naturally ask:

- What if?
- Why not?
- What's possible?
- How could this be different?
- What are we missing?

That mindset can become powerful in:

- entrepreneurship
- leadership
- innovation
- advocacy
- artistic creation
- crisis response

The ADHD brain often struggles to stay emotionally invested in tasks that feel repetitive, stagnant, or disconnected from meaning.

But give the nervous system:

- possibility
- urgency
- meaning
- challenge
- creativity

and suddenly the brain comes alive.

That activation can become extraordinary.

The same person who once struggled through routine classroom tasks may later:

- build companies
- lead movements
- write books
- create art
- transform systems
- emotionally inspire millions

The problem was often not capability.

The problem was environment.

◈

The Relationship Between Pain and Greatness

Many people with ADHD develop extraordinary resilience because life has required them to adapt again and again.

Repeated criticism can teach awareness.

Repeated rejection can sharpen emotional perception.

Repeated struggle can teach reinvention.

Pain changes people.

Especially people who feel life intensely.

Many individuals with ADHD become:

- highly empathetic
- emotionally intuitive
- socially perceptive
- psychologically insightful

because their nervous systems have spent years scanning environments emotionally.

Watching for:

- tone changes

- facial expressions
- emotional shifts
- social tension
- rejection cues

That hyperawareness often develops through emotional survival.

But over time, it can also become:

- intuition
- empathy
- therapeutic ability
- leadership sensitivity
- emotional intelligence

Many extraordinary therapists, teachers, advocates, writers, artists, and recovery leaders may have developed part of their emotional depth through years of navigating intense inner worlds themselves.

That does not romanticize suffering.

But suffering can sometimes sharpen perception.

And ADHD nervous systems often experience life with extraordinary emotional intensity.

◈

The Entrepreneurial Nervous System

Many entrepreneurs may carry ADHD traits.

Not because ADHD guarantees success.

But because entrepreneurship can reward many ADHD strengths:

- creativity
- adaptability
- urgency response
- emotional investment

- risk tolerance
- innovation
- vision
- resilience

Many people with ADHD emotionally suffocate inside rigid systems, yet become fully alive when they are building something meaningful themselves.

Meaning changes nervous system activation.

Purpose changes dopamine engagement.

Passion changes focus.

That distinction can become life-changing.

Many people with ADHD are not incapable of sustained effort.

They are often unable to sustain effort toward environments that feel emotionally disconnected from meaning.

Once meaning appears, the nervous system ignites.

Energy increases.

Ideas increase.

Focus increases.

Creativity increases.

This is why many people with ADHD repeatedly reinvent themselves throughout life.

The nervous system keeps searching for:

- aliveness
- movement
- emotional engagement
- possibility

Without regulation, that search can become destructive.

But when harnessed properly, it can become transformational.

◈

The Emotional Fuel Behind Greatness

Many people misunderstand ambition in individuals with ADHD.

Sometimes ambition is not about ego.

Sometimes ambition is about survival.

Achievement becomes proof that the person is not:

- lazy
- stupid
- broken
- failing

Many people with ADHD become consumed with proving themselves because they spent years feeling misunderstood.

The child who was criticized becomes the adult who overachieves compulsively.

The emotionally dysregulated child becomes the hyperproductive adult who is terrified of failure.

Over time, the nervous system learns a powerful pattern:

Achievement creates validation.

Validation creates dopamine.

Dopamine creates temporary relief.

That cycle can become psychologically addictive, especially among high-functioning adults.

Many adults with ADHD become attached to:

- productivity
- urgency
- achievement
- proving themselves
- external validation

Because stopping forces them to feel everything underneath the movement:

- shame
- exhaustion
- self-doubt
- emotional overwhelm
- fear of inadequacy

That emotional reality can drive brilliant people beyond healthy nervous system limits.

And eventually, many discover something success alone cannot fix:

Achievement does not regulate the nervous system.

◈

Why So Many ADHD Individuals Feel Misunderstood

Many people with ADHD spend years feeling emotionally disconnected from those around them.

Not because they lack social awareness.

Often because they feel life with unusual intensity.

They think deeply.

Love intensely.

React strongly.

Imagine vividly.

Worry deeply.

Care fiercely.

And because society often rewards emotional restraint, many emotionally intense people begin to see themselves as defective.

This can be especially complicated for boys and men.

Many boys with ADHD are taught very early:

- stop crying
- stop overreacting
- calm down
- toughen up

But emotional dysregulation is often neurological.

Not moral.

Many boys grow into men who learn to suppress intensity instead of regulating it.

Over time, that suppression may turn into:

- anger
- emotional shutdown
- substances
- work addiction
- isolation
- impulsivity
- burnout

Women with ADHD may experience different forms of invalidation.

Many high-functioning women become experts at:

- masking
- people pleasing
- perfectionism
- emotional accommodation

while privately drowning in:

- overwhelm
- anxiety
- shame
- overstimulation
- nervous system exhaustion

The tragedy is that many emotionally intense people with ADHD spend years believing they are "too much."

In reality, many were never taught how to regulate nervous systems built for enormous emotional volume.

◈

The Creativity Nobody Could Teach

Many people with ADHD possess creativity that cannot be standardized.

It cannot always be measured through grades.

Or routines.

Or ordinary systems.

Creativity is often nonlinear, and the ADHD mind constantly:

- imagines
- associates
- explores
- reinvents
- questions
- experiments

This kind of creative wiring often produces:

- artists
- musicians
- performers
- writers
- inventors
- storytellers
- visionaries

Many people with ADHD feel most alive while creating because creation powerfully stimulates the nervous system.

That stimulation can become regulating.

For a moment, the person finally feels:

- focused
- engaged
- mentally alive
- purposeful

For some individuals, creativity becomes survival.

The art keeps them emotionally alive.

The music keeps them emotionally alive.

The writing keeps them emotionally alive.

The purpose keeps them emotionally alive.

That connection becomes deeply important in recovery, healing, and identity formation.

Because many people with ADHD eventually discover something they were never taught:

Their nervous system was not designed merely to survive.

It was designed to create.

◈

The Fire That Burns and Builds

Fire gives warmth.

Fire gives light.

Fire transforms what it touches.

But without containment, fire destroys.

That may be one of the clearest metaphors for the ADHD nervous system.

There is often extraordinary psychological fire inside it:

- intensity
- creativity

- imagination
- urgency
- emotional depth
- innovation
- passion
- vision

With regulation, that fire can become power.

But without:

- boundaries
- healing
- self-awareness
- nervous system balance
- emotional regulation

the same fire can begin to damage:

- relationships
- physical health
- emotional stability
- identity
- peace
- sleep
- recovery

Many people with ADHD spend years living between brilliance and burnout.

Feeling simultaneously:

- gifted and exhausted
- visionary and overwhelmed
- emotionally alive and emotionally drowning
- powerful and dysregulated

That contradiction is not weakness.

It is the reality of a nervous system capable of extraordinary possibility while also carrying extraordinary vulnerability.

And understanding that contradiction may be one of the most important things this book can offer.

Because ADHD is not simply:

- a superpower
- or a disorder

It is both more complex and more human than that.

It is fire that can illuminate, create, and transform.

But without grounding, it can also consume the person carrying it.

And learning how to hold both truths honestly, without shame, may become one of the deepest forms of healing an electric mind can experience.

CHAPTER SEVEN

Every Word Felt Personal

Rejection Sensitivity Dysphoria and the ADHD Nervous System

"Are you even listening to me?"

The room changed instantly.

Not physically.

Emotionally.

Jodie wasn't screaming.

She wasn't throwing things.

She had not even said anything cruel.

But the moment those words left her mouth, his nervous system erupted.

The kitchen suddenly felt too quiet.

Too bright.

Too sharp.

The hum of the refrigerator became deafening. The clock on the wall seemed to grow louder. Even the silence between them felt unbearable.

And immediately, the spiral began.

Here we go again.

She's tired of me.

I forgot something again.

I ruined the night.

Why can't I just be normal?

Why do I always do this?

It happened fast.

Too fast.

That is what many people do not understand about rejection sensitivity dysphoria.

The emotional reaction does not build slowly or logically.

It detonates.

One sentence.

One look.

One disappointed sigh.

And suddenly, the nervous system responds as though emotional survival itself is under threat.

Jodie stood at the sink, exhausted after a long day. She had simply been trying to explain something important. But halfway through the conversation, his attention drifted.

Not because he did not care.

That was the painful part.

He cared deeply.

For two seconds, his brain had latched onto something else: a thought about work, a reminder about an email, anxiety about tomorrow. By the time his attention returned to the conversation, Jodie had already noticed the disconnect.

Most couples experience moments like this.

But rejection sensitivity dysphoria can transform an ordinary moment into an emotional avalanche.

Because internally, the ADHD nervous system may not hear:

"You got distracted."

It hears:

"You are failing the people you love again."

That emotional translation happens instantly.

Automatically.

Before logic has time to intervene, shame floods the body.

His chest tightened.

Heat rushed to his face.

His stomach dropped.

His thoughts began racing.

And beneath the defensiveness rising in his voice was something far more painful:

Terror.

Not terror of the argument.

Terror of disappointing someone he loved.

That is what many people never see beneath intense ADHD emotional reactions.

The fear.

The panic.

The shame.

The overwhelming belief that, once again, you have become too much for someone who matters to you.

What made it worse was that one part of his mind understood that the reaction was larger than the situation.

Another part of him could not stop it.

That is the brutal reality of rejection sensitivity dysphoria.

The person may recognize that the emotional reaction is disproportionate.

Yet the nervous system responds as though the pain is life-threatening.

That contradiction creates enormous suffering.

Because afterward comes the self-awareness.

The replaying.

The shame spiral.

The question:

"Why did I react like that?"

Eventually, many people with ADHD begin to fear their own emotions.

Not because they are dangerous.

But because they are emotionally exhausted from feeling everything so intensely.

◈

The Drive Home

The worst part of rejection sensitivity is not always the moment itself.

Sometimes, it is what happens afterward.

The replaying.

The drive home after the conversation.

The silence that follows.

The way the nervous system refuses to let the moment go.

Many people with ADHD replay emotional interactions obsessively.

Not because they are being dramatic.

Because their nervous systems keep searching for resolution.

A simple conversation can become an emotional autopsy that lasts for hours.

Every word is replayed.

Every shift in tone is analyzed.

Every facial expression is revisited.

The mind searches desperately for emotional certainty.

Did I upset them?

Do they still love me?

Are they disappointed in me?

Did I ruin everything?

And because many people with ADHD already carry years of accumulated shame, the nervous system can attach a present rejection to every rejection that came before it.

That is why the emotional response can feel so enormous.

The nervous system is not responding only to the present moment.

It is responding to:

- childhood criticism
- school humiliation
- relationship wounds
- parental disappointment
- social rejection
- past failures
- accumulated shame

All at once.

That emotional stacking can become overwhelming.

Especially because the people around them may see only the current interaction.

They don't see the lifetime of emotional bruises beneath it.

◈

The Child Sitting at the Kitchen Table

Long before adulthood, long before marriage, long before graduate school and professional titles… there was a little boy sitting at a kitchen table, staring at his report card.

The room felt heavy.

His mother looked disappointed.

Not cruel.

Not abusive.

Just tired.

Confused.

Frustrated.

The comments on the report card hurt more than the grades themselves.

"Very intelligent but easily distracted."

"Needs to focus."

"Talks too much."

"Not reaching his potential."

That phrase stayed with him for years.

Not reaching his potential.

The child did not fully understand executive dysfunction.

He did not understand dopamine.

He did not understand nervous system dysregulation.

He understood only one thing:

Somehow, he kept disappointing people, even though he was trying harder than they realized.

When children repeatedly experience correction that feels tied to who they are, the nervous system can begin developing emotional hypervigilance.

The child starts scanning constantly.

Watching for:

- changes in facial expression
- shifts in tone
- emotional reactions
- signs of disappointment

Trying desperately to detect rejection before it arrives.

That hypervigilance becomes a form of survival.

Because once shame attaches itself to identity, the nervous system begins preparing for emotional pain before anything has even happened.

This may help explain why so many people with ADHD become highly attuned to the emotions of others later in life.

They spent years studying the signs of emotional danger.

◈

The Classroom Humiliation

Many people underestimate how emotionally traumatic school can be for children with ADHD.

Especially emotionally sensitive children.

Imagine sitting in class, already trying harder than anyone realizes.

Trying not to move too much.

Trying not to interrupt.

Trying not to drift away mentally.

Trying not to forget the instructions.

Trying not to get in trouble again.

Then, without warning, the teacher says:

"Joseph, pay attention."

Every face turns toward him.

Heat rushes through his body.

Embarrassment takes over.

And even if no one else remembers the moment the next day, his nervous system may carry it for years.

That is one of the painful realities of rejection sensitivity.

Emotionally charged moments can leave a deep imprint.

Especially public embarrassment.

Especially shame.

Especially criticism.

Many adults with ADHD can still vividly remember childhood moments when they:

- felt stupid
- were laughed at
- were corrected publicly
- disappointed a teacher
- forgot an assignment
- felt socially rejected

Not because they are weak.

Because emotionally intense experiences can be encoded with unusual depth.

Researchers are still examining the mechanisms associated with rejection sensitivity dysphoria, but many people with ADHD describe strikingly similar patterns:

- emotional flooding after criticism
- intense fear of rejection
- overwhelming shame spirals
- reactions that feel difficult to control
- obsessive replaying of conflict
- people-pleasing
- avoidance

Clinicians such as William Dodson have written and spoken extensively about rejection sensitivity in people with ADHD because these patterns frequently appear in clinical settings.

And when people finally discover language for what they have been experiencing, many become overwhelmed with emotion.

Not because they are weak.

Because, for the first time in their lives, their pain finally makes sense.

◈

The Graduate School Breakdown

High-functioning people with ADHD often become exceptionally skilled at hiding rejection sensitivity.

Especially academically and professionally.

The outside world sees:

- achievement
- intelligence
- professionalism
- leadership

But internally, the nervous system may be carrying:

- panic
- self-doubt
- shame
- emotional hypervigilance

Returning to graduate school later in life brought rejection sensitivity into sharper focus.

A professor critiques a paper.

Objectively, the feedback is normal.

Appropriate.

Part of the academic process.

But internally, the response can feel overwhelming.

Suddenly:

- self-worth collapses
- shame floods the body
- imposter syndrome takes over
- panic begins to rise

And while the person may appear calm in class, the mind is spiraling beneath the surface:

I don't belong here.

Everyone else is smarter than I am.

I am failing.

Eventually, they will realize I am not good enough.

This hidden collapse is one reason high-functioning adults with ADHD can become so emotionally exhausted.

Their nervous systems are constantly fighting battles no one else can see.

And because they have learned to appear composed, others assume they are coping well.

Meanwhile, internally, they may be:

- replaying criticism for days
- obsessing over mistakes
- spiraling emotionally
- questioning their worth

Achievement does not erase rejection sensitivity.

In some cases, it intensifies it.

Because the more deeply someone cares about succeeding, the more devastating criticism can feel.

◈

The Relationship Between Shame and Rage

One of the least understood expressions of rejection sensitivity is anger.

Not cruelty.

Not abuse.

Emotional overload.

For some people with ADHD, shame can turn into defensiveness or rage almost instantly.

Especially when they feel:

- criticized
- misunderstood
- rejected
- emotionally cornered
- invalidated

The nervous system can become overwhelmed so quickly that the reaction occurs before logical thought has time to intervene.

The person may become:

- reactive
- defensive
- emotionally explosive
- withdrawn
- shut down

Then comes the guilt.

The shame.

The self-hatred.

The question:

Why do I keep reacting this way?

Many emotionally sensitive people with ADHD are deeply distressed by the possibility of hurting others.

That makes the aftermath of dysregulation even more painful.

The nervous system reacts intensely, then punishes itself relentlessly.

Over time, that cycle becomes psychologically exhausting.

◈

The People Pleaser

Many people with ADHD become chronic people-pleasers.

Not because they lack an identity.

Because rejection can feel emotionally catastrophic.

The nervous system begins to learn:

Approval means safety.

Disappointment means danger.

So the person starts:

- apologizing constantly
- overexplaining
- suppressing their needs
- avoiding conflict
- masking their emotions
- overperforming
- overgiving

All in an effort to prevent rejection.

This pattern may be especially common among:

- trauma survivors
- high-functioning women
- caregivers
- emotionally sensitive people
- professionals

Eventually, the person becomes exhausted from managing everyone else's emotional comfort while quietly abandoning their own.

And over time, they may no longer know who they are beneath the performance.

◈

Why Rejection Feels Physically Painful

One of the most validating discoveries for many people with ADHD is learning that emotional pain can activate real neurological pathways.

Research on social rejection has found overlap between the brain systems involved in processing emotional and physical pain.

This does not mean rejection sensitivity is imagined or exaggerated.

It means emotional threat can be experienced intensely throughout the nervous system and body.

Many people describe rejection through physical sensations such as:

- tightness in the chest
- a dropping sensation in the stomach
- sudden heat
- panic
- emotional paralysis
- a sense of nervous system flooding

The body can react before logic has time to intervene.

That is why telling someone in a state of emotional dysregulation to simply "calm down" often does not help.

The nervous system may already be responding as though it is in danger.

◈

The Fear of Being Too Much

At the center of rejection sensitivity often lies one terrifying fear:

Eventually, everyone will realize I am too much.

Too emotional.

Too forgetful.

Too intense.

Too sensitive.

Too overwhelming.

Too difficult.

That fear shapes countless lives.

Many people with ADHD spend years:

- shrinking themselves
- masking
- suppressing their emotions
- overperforming
- becoming hyper-independent

All in an effort to avoid becoming an emotional burden.

Beneath these behaviors often lies a profound fear of abandonment.

A fear of disappointing others.

A fear of losing connection.

Living with that fear is exhausting because the nervous system rarely relaxes socially.

It remains alert.

Constantly scanning for signs of emotional danger.

◈

Healing the Invisible Bruise

Healing rejection sensitivity is not about becoming emotionless.

It is about learning how to regulate intense emotional responses safely.

That may involve developing:

- emotional awareness
- self-compassion
- communication skills
- healthy boundaries
- resilience to shame
- nervous system regulation

- emotional pacing

Many people with ADHD have spent years surviving their emotions.

Few were ever taught how to regulate them.

That distinction changes everything.

Healing often begins when someone finally realizes:

There is a reason I react this way.

Not an excuse.

An explanation.

And an explanation can loosen the grip of shame.

Many people benefit from forms of support such as:

- trauma-informed therapy
- ADHD-informed therapy
- mindfulness practices
- nervous system regulation exercises
- emotional regulation strategies
- safe and supportive relationships
- consistent sleep routines
- deeper self-understanding

Most importantly, healing begins when people stop seeing themselves as broken simply because they feel deeply.

Emotional intensity is not weakness.

The nervous system may simply never have learned how to carry that intensity safely.

◈

Every Word Felt Personal

That may be the simplest way to describe rejection sensitivity dysphoria:

Every word felt personal.

Every criticism felt enormous.

Every disappointment felt catastrophic.

Every look seemed loaded with meaning.

For many people with ADHD, life becomes emotionally exhausting because the nervous system never stops searching for signs of rejection.

That exhaustion is often invisible.

But invisibility does not make the suffering any less real.

Millions of people quietly carry:

- the overthinking
- the shame spirals
- the emotional flooding
- the panic after criticism
- the fear of disappointing others
- the fear of abandonment
- the fear of being too much

Perhaps the most heartbreaking part is that many people who struggle with rejection sensitivity are also deeply caring, emotionally devoted, and empathetic.

They often feel deeply because they care deeply.

The problem is not the depth of feeling itself.

The nervous system simply may not have learned how to regulate that intensity safely.

But understanding can change everything.

Because when people finally realize:

I am not crazy.

I am not weak.

I am not broken.

Shame begins to loosen its grip.

And perhaps, for the first time in their lives, they can stop hating themselves for how deeply they feel.

CHAPTER EIGHT

The War Between Chaos and Control ⚡

ADHD, Addiction, and the Search for Relief

Some people use substances to get high.

Others use them because, for the first time in their lives, everything inside them grows quiet.

The racing thoughts slow.

The emotional intensity softens.

The nervous system finally releases its grip.

That distinction matters.

For many people with ADHD, addiction is not simply about partying, rebellion, recklessness, or a lack of discipline.

Often, it begins as a search for relief.

Relief from:

- overstimulation
- emotional flooding
- racing thoughts
- shame
- rejection sensitivity
- anxiety

- nervous system exhaustion
- internal chaos

The outside world sees the substance.

The behavior.

The consequences.

What it rarely sees is the nervous system beneath them.

The child who could never slow down.

The teenager who never learned how emotional regulation was supposed to feel.

The adult whose mind never stayed quiet long enough to rest.

Then, one day, something makes the noise stop.

For some, it's alcohol.

For others, relief may come through:

- opioids
- stimulants
- benzodiazepines
- marijuana
- cocaine
- gambling
- sex
- work
- shopping
- chaos itself

The substance or behavior may change.

The need beneath it often remains the same.

A need for quiet.

For escape.

For regulation.

For even a few moments of relief from a nervous system that never seems to power down.

Before anyone can fully understand the relationship between ADHD and addiction, they must first understand what it can feel like to live inside that constant internal noise.

◈

The First Time the Noise Stopped

The first experience did not feel dangerous.

That matters.

Most people imagine addiction beginning with recklessness.

But for many people with ADHD, it begins with emotional relief so profound that it can feel almost spiritual.

The first time the nervous system slows down can feel life-changing.

For the first time:

- the thoughts soften
- the tension eases
- the emotional pain grows quieter
- the anxiety fades
- the shame briefly loosens its grip

And suddenly, the person experiences something they may never have known consistently before:

Peace.

Not happiness.

Peace.

That moment can leave a powerful neurological and emotional imprint.

Especially for someone who has spent years drowning in internal noise.

Many people with ADHD do not initially experience substances only as euphoric.

They experience them as regulating.

That distinction matters clinically.

Because, at first, the person may not be chasing destruction.

They may be chasing relief.

Research has consistently found an increased risk of substance use disorders among people with ADHD, particularly when ADHD remains untreated. Authors and clinicians such as Gabor Maté and Edward M. Hallowell have also explored the connections among emotional dysregulation, dopamine functioning, impulsivity, and vulnerability to addiction.

The ADHD nervous system may continually search for stimulation, regulation, or escape.

Substances can temporarily provide all three.

And that relief can become emotionally unforgettable.

◈

The Dopamine Chase

To understand why people with ADHD may be vulnerable to addiction, it is important to understand dopamine.

Dopamine is often described as the brain's "pleasure chemical."

But its role is far more complex.

Dopamine is involved in:

- motivation
- reward processing
- anticipation
- attention regulation
- novelty-seeking
- emotional engagement
- reinforcement learning

ADHD is associated with differences in the brain systems involved in dopamine signaling and reward processing.

As a result, many people with ADHD may struggle with:

- under-stimulation
- inconsistent reward processing
- regulating motivation
- sustaining engagement

This may help explain why so many people with ADHD experience persistent internal restlessness.

The nervous system keeps searching for:

- stimulation
- novelty
- intensity
- urgency
- emotional activation

Substances can produce rapid changes in mood, arousal, and reward.

That immediacy creates powerful reinforcement.

The brain learns:

"This makes me feel better now."

That lesson can become dangerous.

Especially for someone already carrying:

- shame
- rejection sensitivity
- trauma
- anxiety
- chronic overwhelm

Over time, the nervous system may begin chasing relief compulsively.

Not because the person lacks morality or discipline.

Because the brain has learned to associate relief with survival.

◈

The Child Who Never Felt Calm

Many people who later struggle with addiction can trace their emotional dysregulation back to childhood.

The inability to settle internally.

The constant restlessness.

The emotional intensity.

The overstimulation.

The feeling of never being able to fully relax.

Many children with ADHD spend years hearing:

- calm down
- sit still
- stop overreacting
- focus
- why are you acting like this?

But few are taught:

- how to regulate their nervous systems
- how to recognize and understand their emotions
- how to manage sensory overload
- how to soothe themselves safely
- how to work with executive functioning challenges

The child learns correction.

Not regulation.

That distinction can shape an entire life.

Because many of these children eventually become adults whose nervous systems still do not know how to settle safely.

Then, one day, a substance creates temporary calm.

The thoughts slow.

The tension releases.

The internal chaos grows quiet.

That relief can create a powerful emotional attachment.

Especially for someone who has spent years feeling ashamed of how chaotic life feels inside.

The substance begins to represent:

- escape
- relief
- quiet
- confidence
- numbness
- regulation

At first, it feels like a solution.

Eventually, it can begin to feel like survival.

◈

The Double Life

One of the cruelest realities of ADHD and addiction is that many people become exceptionally skilled at functioning on the outside while privately falling apart.

Especially intelligent people.

Professionals.

Caregivers.

The world sees:

- success
- leadership
- charisma
- productivity
- intelligence

But beneath that performance, the nervous system may be surviving through:

- substances
- overwork
- chaos
- adrenaline
- emotional suppression

Many people with ADHD become masters of appearing capable.

Masking.

Overcompensating.

Managing how others see them.

Because the shame of being exposed can feel unbearable.

Over time, the person begins living two lives:

- the identity presented to the world
- the private struggle to survive

Maintaining both becomes exhausting.

The person must protect the image, conceal the addiction, manage the consequences, and continue performing as though nothing is wrong.

Eventually, the weight of that divided life becomes psychologically devastating.

◈

The Shame Spiral

Shame can become one of the strongest forces sustaining addiction.

Especially ADHD addiction.

Many people with ADHD grow up believing:

- something is wrong with them
- they always disappoint others

- they are failing
- they are too emotional
- they are too impulsive
- they are too much

Substances can temporarily interrupt that shame.

For a brief moment:

- self-hatred grows quieter
- overthinking slows
- emotional pain softens

That interruption can become deeply reinforcing.

But eventually, the substance begins creating another layer of shame.

Now the person may be carrying:

- shame about the addiction
- shame about ADHD
- shame about damaged relationships
- shame about perceived failure
- shame about secrecy

The nervous system becomes trapped between the pain that drives the behavior and the shame the behavior creates.

Over time, many people begin to believe they are permanently broken.

That hopelessness can be dangerous.

And recovery may become more difficult when ADHD remains untreated and the underlying patterns of impulsivity, emotional dysregulation, and stimulation-seeking are never addressed.

◈

The High-Functioning Addict

Many people still understand addiction through stereotypes.

Homelessness.

Arrests.

Public collapse.

Visible destruction.

But many people with ADHD who struggle with addiction remain outwardly functional for years.

Sometimes for decades.

Hyperfocus, adrenaline, intelligence, and relentless overcompensation can help sustain the appearance of control.

The person may remain:

- productive
- successful
- professionally respected
- socially charismatic

while privately deteriorating.

This can be especially dangerous because high-functioning people are often among the last to receive help.

Their success conceals the severity of the struggle.

Their responsibilities continue to be met.

Their performance remains convincing.

So no one sees the collapse unfolding behind closed doors.

And because many people with ADHD become highly skilled at masking emotional pain, they may suffer in silence while appearing composed and successful.

The exhaustion becomes indescribable.

Each day is lived with the fear that:

- someone will discover the truth
- the mask will crack
- the performance will collapse

That fear can keep people trapped in addiction far longer than anyone around them realizes.

Recovery and the ADHD Nervous System

One of the most misunderstood realities of recovery is this: getting sober does not automatically regulate the nervous system.

The substance is removed.

The ADHD remains.

For many people, this becomes painfully clear during early recovery.

Once the substance is gone, the symptoms it may have temporarily numbed, quieted, or concealed can become impossible to ignore:

- racing thoughts
- emotional flooding
- impulsivity
- restlessness
- rejection sensitivity
- overstimulation
- executive dysfunction

Some people relapse not because they do not want recovery, but because they have not yet learned how to live sober inside a nervous system that still feels chaotic.

That distinction matters deeply.

Recovery requires more than the desire to stop using.

It also requires tools for managing the pain, dysregulation, and unmet needs that the substance once helped suppress.

Untreated ADHD may complicate recovery by leaving patterns.

Writers and clinicians, including Gabor Maté, have emphasized the importance of understanding the emotional pain beneath compulsive behavior rather than focusing only on condemning the behavior itself.

For many people, recovery involves learning:

- emotional regulation
- nervous system regulation
- self-awareness
- structure and routine
- sustainable pacing
- emotional processing
- executive functioning strategies

Not only abstinence.

Healing requires far more than removing substances.

It requires learning how to live inside the nervous system safely..

◈

When Recovery Becomes Purpose

Many people with ADHD become powerful forces within recovery communities.

Not despite their ADHD.

Sometimes because of it.

The same nervous system that once chased chaos can become deeply committed to:

- healing
- advocacy
- service
- leadership
- transformation
- connection
- purpose

A sense of purpose can have a powerful regulating effect.

Meaning offers a form of motivation that substances cannot provide.

Connection creates grounding.

Service builds an identity beyond addiction and shame.

Over time, many people in recovery realize that the intensity that once nearly destroyed them can also become the force that helps save lives.

That realization can be profoundly emotional.

Many have spent years believing their intensity could only create destruction.

Then, gradually, they begin to see something different:

- their empathy helps others heal
- their emotional depth creates connection
- their honesty builds trust
- their passion inspires others
- their pain becomes purpose

That is one of the most meaningful transformations possible within the ADHD recovery journey.

◈

The Stigma Around Medication

One of the most complex conversations surrounding ADHD and addiction involves medication.

Especially stimulant medication.

The stigma can be intense.

Some people believe stimulant treatment is inherently dangerous for anyone with a history of addiction.

Others argue that leaving ADHD untreated may create its own risks, including greater impulsivity, emotional dysregulation, and vulnerability to relapse.

The reality is more nuanced.

Evidence suggests that appropriately prescribed and carefully monitored ADHD treatment can improve functioning and reduce certain risk behaviors for many people.

At the same time, treatment must remain individualized, ethical, trauma-informed, and closely supervised.

There is no single approach that works for everyone.

Some people benefit significantly from stimulant medication.

Others may respond better to:

- non-stimulant medication
- psychotherapy
- behavioral interventions
- exercise
- mindfulness practices
- nervous system regulation strategies

The larger point is this:

Conversations about ADHD treatment must become more compassionate, evidence-informed, and free from unnecessary shame.

Because stigma can prevent people from seeking the care they need.

◈

The War Between Chaos and Control

Many people with ADHD spend years caught between two opposing needs:

Chaos.

Control.

One part of the nervous system craves:

- stimulation

- urgency
- intensity
- novelty
- emotional activation

Another part longs for:

- peace
- structure
- regulation
- consistency
- calm

Living between those competing needs can be exhausting.

Many people genuinely want stability, yet begin to feel restless, disconnected, or emotionally under-stimulated when life becomes too predictable.

That contradiction can be difficult for others to understand.

But it reflects dysregulation more than a lack of discipline or commitment.

Healing often involves learning how to build a life that is:

- stimulating without becoming destructive
- structured without becoming emotionally restrictive
- emotionally alive without becoming chaotic

The goal is not to eliminate intensity.

It is to create enough safety and structure for that intensity to become sustainable.

Finding that balance can change a life.

◈

The Person Underneath the Disorder

Perhaps the most heartbreaking part of addiction stigma is how quickly people stop seeing the human being beneath the behavior.

This can be especially painful for people with ADHD.

The world sees:

- impulsivity
- emotional intensity
- inconsistency
- addiction
- chaos

But beneath those struggles may be:

- pain
- sensitivity
- emotional depth
- intelligence
- shame
- exhaustion
- a longing for peace

People with ADHD who struggle with addiction are not broken.

They are often overwhelmed people whose nervous systems have been searching desperately for a way to survive.

Understanding this does not remove personal responsibility.

It creates a more honest foundation for it.

Compassion and accountability are not opposites.

Lasting healing often requires both.

◈

The Search for Peace

At its core, addiction often begins as a search.

A search for:

- relief
- quiet

- connection
- calm
- escape
- regulation
- peace

For many people with ADHD, that search becomes deeply personal after years of living with relentless internal intensity.

The tragedy is that many discover substances before they discover healthier ways to regulate themselves.

Chaos before healing.

Numbing before understanding.

Relief before recovery.

But recovery opens another possibility.

Over time, many people begin to understand that lasting peace cannot come from a substance alone.

It must also be built within the nervous system.

Emotionally.

Spiritually.

Relationally.

And as the nervous system gradually learns what genuine safety and regulation feel like, something extraordinary can happen:

The same electric mind that once carried a person toward destruction can become a source of healing.

For themselves.

And for others.

PART III

ESCAPE, ADDICTION & COLLAPSE

CHAPTER NINE

The Noise Never Stopped

ADHD, Addiction, and the Search for Silence

I just wanted my head to shut up.

That was all.

I did not want to die.

I did not want to destroy my life.

I did not want to become addicted.

I just wanted silence.

That was the part no one understood.

By the time substances entered my life, the war inside my mind had already been raging for years.

The racing thoughts.

The emotional chaos.

The constant restlessness.

The feeling that my nervous system was plugged into an electrical outlet twenty-four hours a day.

I remember lying in bed at night, staring into the darkness, physically exhausted but mentally wide awake.

My body begged for sleep.

My mind refused.

Thoughts crashed into one another.

Conversations replayed.

Shame resurfaced.

Embarrassing moments returned in sharp detail.

Fears about the future collided with memories from childhood.

Everything came at once.

It always came at once.

People without ADHD often imagine distraction as simple forgetfulness.

They do not understand the noise.

The internal static.

The emotional overstimulation.

The exhaustion of living inside a mind that never stays quiet long enough to rest.

And after living inside that kind of nervous system for years, relief stops feeling optional.

It begins to feel necessary.

I did not understand dopamine.

I did not understand emotional dysregulation.

I did not understand executive dysfunction.

I did not understand nervous system overstimulation.

I understood only this:

Something inside me never stopped moving.

Eventually, I found substances that could make it stop.

Temporarily.

The first time everything slowed down felt almost spiritual.

Not euphoric.

Not exciting.

Quiet.

For the first time in my life, my brain was no longer attacking me.

The noise softened.

The tension released.

The panic loosened its grip.

The emotional static faded into the background.

And suddenly, one terrifying thought came to me:

This must be what normal feels like.

That kind of relief can change a person.

Especially someone living with emotional dysregulation.

Especially someone with ADHD.

Especially someone carrying ADHD alongside trauma, shame, rejection, emotional flooding, overstimulation, and exhaustion.

Because when a nervous system finally experiences relief after years of internal chaos, the attachment to that relief can form quickly.

Powerfully.

Dangerously.

◈

The Boy Nobody Could Slow Down

Long before heroin.

Long before opiates.

Long before addiction became visible, there was a little boy whose nervous system never seemed to rest.

Teachers saw:

- hyperactivity
- impulsivity
- emotional intensity
- distractibility

But beneath those behaviors was something deeper:

a child who did not know how to regulate what was happening inside him.

The world kept telling him to:

- calm down
- focus
- stop overreacting
- sit still
- stop interrupting
- stop being so emotional

But no one taught him:

- how to regulate his nervous system
- how to understand and manage his emotions
- how to cope with sensory overload
- how to soothe himself safely
- how to work with executive functioning challenges

He learned shame before he learned regulation.

That difference can shape an entire life.

Over time, many children with ADHD begin to see themselves as:

- failures
- disappointments
- problems
- burdens
- too much

That shame settles deep.

And when shame becomes chronic, the nervous system begins searching for somewhere to escape.

Some children find refuge in:

- sports
- art

- music
- performance
- achievement

Others eventually find substances.

And substances work quickly.

That is what makes them so dangerous.

◈

The First Time the Brain Went Quiet

People who have never lived with severe nervous system dysregulation may misunderstand addiction entirely.

They see recklessness.

Bad decisions.

Weakness.

But for many people with ADHD, the first experience with a substance may feel very different.

Less like intoxication.

More like relief.

When opiates first entered the nervous system, something happened that felt almost impossible to explain.

Everything slowed down.

Not around him.

Inside him.

The thoughts softened.

The anxiety receded.

The emotional pain disappeared temporarily.

The nervous system finally stopped screaming.

And after years of internal chaos, that silence can become addictive.

Because, at first, many people with ADHD are not chasing destruction.

They are chasing regulation.

Writers and clinicians such as Gabor Maté have explored how addiction can develop as an attempt to escape emotional pain, trauma, dysregulation, and chronic nervous system distress.

That perspective matters when discussing ADHD.

Many people with ADHD live with overwhelming internal intensity long before addiction becomes visible to anyone else.

The substance may initially provide:

- relief
- emotional anesthesia
- nervous system quiet
- temporary regulation
- escape from shame

At first, it feels like relief.

Over time, it can begin to feel like survival.

◈

The Dopamine Starvation

To understand why people with ADHD may be vulnerable to addiction, it is important to understand dopamine.

Dopamine is not simply about pleasure.

It plays an important role in:

- reward
- motivation
- anticipation
- attention
- emotional engagement

- reinforcement
- drive

ADHD is associated with differences in the brain systems involved in dopamine signaling, motivation, and reward processing.

As a result, many people with ADHD may struggle with:

- under-stimulation
- inconsistent reward processing
- persistent restlessness
- difficulty regulating motivation
- The nervous system keeps searching for:
- novelty
- stimulation
- excitement
- urgency
- emotional activation

That constant search can become exhausting.

Substances can produce rapid changes in dopamine.

The brain learns:

This works immediately.

That lesson can become deeply reinforcing.

Especially for someone already carrying:

- emotional pain
- rejection sensitivity
- trauma
- chronic shame
- anxiety
- nervous system exhaustion

Over time, substance use may stop feeling recreational.

The nervous system begins relying on it as a way to regulate distress, quiet internal noise, or feel temporarily steady.

◈

The Trap House Mind

People often imagine addiction beginning somewhere outside the person.

In the streets.

With dealers.

With needles.

With visible chaos.

But addiction often begins long before any of that becomes visible.

It begins inside the mind.

Inside emotional pain.

Inside a nervous system desperate for relief.

By the time the struggle becomes visible to others, the person may have already spent years drowning in private.

Eventually, the substance stops offering relief and begins creating dependence.

That shift can happen gradually.

Then seem to arrive all at once.

The person who once used substances to:

- relax
- escape
- feel confident
- quiet the mind

may one day realize they no longer know how to function without them.

That realization can be terrifying.

Especially for someone already carrying years of shame.

Now the shame multiplies.

The person may begin carrying:

- shame about ADHD
- shame about addiction
- shame about perceived failure
- shame about damaged relationships
- shame about secrecy
- fear
- hopelessness

The substance temporarily relieves the suffering.

Then it creates more suffering.

The pain drives the use, and the use deepens the pain.

That is how the cycle begins feeding itself.

◈

The Double Life

Many high-functioning people with ADHD and addiction become exceptionally skilled at performing competence.

Especially those who are intelligent, socially perceptive, or charismatic.

The outside world sees:

- confidence
- humor
- leadership
- intelligence
- productivity

But beneath that performance, the nervous system may be collapsing.

Living with that contradiction is psychologically exhausting.

Every day carries the fear that:

- someone will discover the truth

- the mask will crack
- the performance will collapse

Many people learn to survive through appearance.

The smiling addict.

The functioning addict.

The successful addict.

That invisibility can become dangerous because support often arrives only after the collapse can no longer be hidden.

But the visible collapse is rarely where the story begins.

Inside, it may have started years earlier.

◈

The Shame That Followed Everything

Shame can become one of addiction's most powerful fuels.

Especially when it is layered with years of ADHD-related shame.

Many people with ADHD grow up carrying:

- feelings of inadequacy
- fear of disappointing others
- rejection sensitivity
- emotional dysregulation
- relentless self-criticism

Substances can temporarily numb those feelings.

Then, over time, they create new reasons for shame.

That cycle can become psychologically devastating.

The person wakes up promising:

I'm done.

Then the nervous system begins screaming again.

The anxiety returns.

The emotional pain returns.

The overstimulation returns.

The shame returns.

Eventually, the need for immediate relief overpowers the promise to stop.

Each return to substance use weakens the person's trust in themselves.

And after enough attempts to quit, many begin to believe they are incapable of recovery.

Hopelessness takes hold.

And hopelessness can become dangerous.

◈

Why Recovery Can Be Harder for People with ADHD

One of the cruelest realities many people discover in recovery is this:

Removing the substance does not automatically resolve the dysregulation beneath it.

The drugs are gone.

The ADHD remains.

For many people, that becomes painfully clear during early sobriety.

Without the substance that once numbed or quieted the nervous system:

- emotions may feel overwhelming
- thoughts may become relentless
- impulses may feel harder to manage
- boredom may feel unbearable
- shame may resurface
- overstimulation may become impossible to ignore

Some people relapse not because they do not want recovery, but because they have not yet learned how to live sober inside a nervous system that still feels chaotic.

That distinction matters.

People with ADHD face an elevated risk of substance use disorders, particularly when ADHD remains untreated or unsupported.

Recovery may also become more difficult when underlying patterns such as impulsivity, emotional dysregulation, executive dysfunction, and stimulation-seeking remain unaddressed.

Meaningful recovery may require:

- emotional regulation skills
- executive functioning support
- nervous system regulation
- trauma-informed care
- appropriate ADHD treatment
- structure and routine
- purpose
- connection
- self-awareness

Not abstinence alone.

Abstinence removes the substance.

It does not automatically heal the shame.

The emotional flooding.

The executive dysfunction.

Or the nervous system patterns that made escape feel necessary.

Healing requires deeper work.

◈

The Search for Meaning

One of the most important shifts in recovery can occur when a person stops asking:

How do I stop using?

and begins asking:

How do I build a life I no longer need to escape from?

That question changes the direction of recovery.

Because, over time, many people with ADHD discover that purpose can provide the nervous system with something substances never could:

A reason to remain present.

Meaning can strengthen motivation.

Connection can create safety.

Service can build self-worth.

Helping others can transform pain into something useful.

Recovery communities can be profoundly healing for people with ADHD because they often provide:

- stimulation
- emotional connection
- structure
- purpose
- accountability
- belonging

For many, recovery becomes the first environment where:

- honesty feels safe
- vulnerability is accepted
- emotional intensity is understood

That matters deeply.

Especially for people who have spent years believing they were:

- too much
- too emotional
- too broken
- too chaotic

In the right community, the very qualities they once learned to hide may become the qualities that help them connect, contribute, and heal.

◈

The Addiction That Was Never Really About Drugs

At its core, addiction is rarely about the substance alone.

This may be especially important to understand in people with ADHD.

Substance use often begins as an attempt to quiet something deeper:

- emotional pain
- nervous system chaos
- overstimulation
- shame
- trauma
- loneliness
- rejection
- exhaustion

The substance becomes a temporary answer to a desperate internal question:

How do I survive inside my own mind and body?

That question deserves compassion.

Not excuses.

Not freedom from accountability.

Compassion.

Because understanding the pain beneath the behavior changes how treatment begins.

And better treatment can change a life.

◈

The Noise Never Stopped

Perhaps that is the clearest way to describe the relationship between ADHD and addiction:

The noise never stopped.

The thoughts.

The emotions.

The overstimulation.

The shame.

The panic.

The restlessness.

The nervous system exhaustion.

Eventually, substances became the only reliable way to quiet that noise for a while.

Then the relief became another source of suffering.

But perhaps the most important truth in this chapter is that many people who survived addiction were never weak.

They were overwhelmed people whose nervous systems had been searching desperately for peace.

Recognizing that does not erase the harm addiction can cause.

It changes the question we ask about it.

Instead of:

What is wrong with you?

we begin asking:

What pain were you trying to quiet, and what made relief feel worth risking everything for? ⚡

CHAPTER TEN

The War Over Treatment

Medication, THC, Psychedelics, Stigma, and the Fight to Be Understood

Few conversations in mental health become louder than the debate over ADHD treatment.

The moment medication enters the discussion, people begin choosing sides.

Stimulants are either "life-saving" or "legal meth."

Cannabis is either "medicine" or "an excuse."

Psychedelics are either "the future" or "dangerous nonsense."

Therapy is either "essential" or "not enough."

Lifestyle changes are either "powerful" or "oversold."

And somewhere beneath all that noise is the person with ADHD.

The child who cannot sit still.

The teenager drowning in shame.

The mother barely functioning beneath the weight of overwhelm.

The executive quietly burning out.

The person in recovery trying to remain sober inside a nervous system that has never known how to settle.

That person does not need a culture war.

They need help.

Compassion.

Options.

Honesty.

They need people to stop weaponizing ignorance and start asking better questions.

Because ADHD treatment should not be about defending a position.

It should be about helping someone function.

Keeping them safe.

Protecting their dignity.

Helping them understand and regulate a nervous system that may have gone unsupported for years.

But stigma has distorted the conversation.

People who have never lived with ADHD often speak with absolute certainty about what someone with the condition should or should not use.

They call medication a weakness.

Cannabis an excuse for laziness.

Psychedelics insanity.

They insist therapy should be enough.

That exercise should fix it.

That discipline should fix it.

That prayer should fix it.

That structure should fix it.

Sometimes, these judgments come from people who understand almost nothing about ADHD itself.

That is dangerous.

Because shame does not treat ADHD.

Stigma does not regulate a nervous system.

Judgment does not repair executive dysfunction.

And moral certainty cannot replace individualized, evidence-informed care.

◈

The Fear of Medication

For many families, the idea of ADHD medication can feel frightening.

Especially stimulant medication.

Parents may wonder:

- Will this change my child?
- Will it affect their personality?
- Could they become dependent on it?
- Is it safe?
- Am I failing as a parent?
- Will other people judge me?

Adults carry fears of their own.

Especially those with a history of addiction.

They may ask:

- Can I trust myself with this medication?
- Could it trigger old patterns?
- Will people assume I am drug-seeking?
- Will my recovery community judge me?
- Am I allowed to need medication?

Those fears are real.

They deserve to be taken seriously.

But fear alone cannot become the treatment plan.

The National Institute of Mental Health describes ADHD treatment as potentially including medication and psychosocial interventions, such as behavioral treatment, parent training, school-based support, and cognitive-behavioral approaches. The CDC similarly notes that treatment for adults may involve medication, psychotherapy, education or training, or a combination of approaches.

That does not mean everyone needs the same kind of treatment.

It means ADHD deserves to be treated with the same seriousness as any other neurodevelopmental condition.

No shame.

No shortcuts.

No automatic condemnation.

No one with ADHD should have to apologize for needing support.

◈

Stimulants: Miracle or Monster?

Few medications carry as much stigma as stimulants prescribed for ADHD.

They are called dangerous.

Addictive.

People call them "legal speed."

And yet, for many people with ADHD, stimulant medication can be life-changing.

Not because it makes them high.

Because, when appropriately prescribed, it may help them regulate attention, impulses, and daily functioning.

For some people, stimulant treatment can improve:

- attention
- impulse control
- task initiation
- emotional regulation
- follow-through

- executive functioning
- day-to-day stability

That does not mean stimulants are risk-free.

They are controlled substances.

They require careful assessment, monitoring, responsible prescribing, and individualized decision-making.

But stigma often obscures an essential truth:

A medication can carry genuine risks and still be clinically appropriate.

Both realities can exist at the same time.

People often want treatment to fit into simple categories.

Safe or dangerous.

Good or bad.

Necessary or unnecessary.

But ADHD treatment is rarely that simple.

Some people function significantly better with stimulants.

Others cannot tolerate them.

Some are at risk of misusing them.

Others benefit more from non-stimulant medication.

Some need medication alongside therapy.

Others may also need structure, coaching, sleep support, exercise, and trauma-informed care.

People with a history of addiction may require additional safeguards, closer monitoring, or alternative treatment options.

None of this makes medication universally good or universally bad.

It means treatment must be tailored to the individual.

That is what thoughtful, responsible clinical care looks like.

◈

The Recovery Question

For people in recovery, ADHD treatment can feel deeply complicated.

This is personal.

After living through addiction, the idea of taking a controlled medication can awaken fear, judgment, and uncertainty.

But recovery communities and clinical systems must also hold another truth carefully:

Leaving ADHD untreated can carry risks of its own.

Untreated or unsupported ADHD may contribute to:

- impulsivity
- emotional dysregulation
- vulnerability to relapse
- disorganization
- shame
- compulsive stimulation-seeking
- difficulty creating and maintaining structure

So the central question cannot be:

Is this medication controversial?

It must be:

What is the safest, most effective, and most ethical treatment plan for this particular person?

For some, that plan may include stimulant medication.

For others, it may involve non-stimulant options.

Depending on the person's needs and history, treatment may also include therapy, coaching, peer support, recovery accountability, psychiatric monitoring, medication agreements, pill counts, or toxicology screening when clinically appropriate.

The goal is not to defend an ideology.

The goal is stability.

A recovery-centered approach to ADHD care should be compassionate, structured, transparent, and clinically informed.

Not driven by fear.

Not shaped by shame.

Not reckless.

Not inflexible.

◈

Non-Stimulants, Therapy, and the Middle Ground

Conversations about ADHD treatment are often dominated by stimulants.

But comprehensive ADHD care extends far beyond a single medication class.

Non-stimulant medications may be appropriate for people who:

- cannot tolerate stimulants
- have certain medical contraindications or risks
- have concerns related to substance use
- experience significant anxiety or sleep difficulties
- prefer a non-controlled medication

Behavioral and psychosocial interventions also play an important role.

Alongside established medication and psychosocial care, NIMH researchers continue to study supportive approaches such as neurofeedback, cognitive training, mindfulness-based interventions, and neuromodulation.

For adults, cognitive-behavioral therapy may help address:

- time management
- organization
- emotional regulation

- procrastination
- negative self-talk
- avoidance
- shame-based patterns

For children, parent training and school-based support can be essential.

Medication may make the brain more available for learning and practicing new skills.

But medication alone cannot do everything.

It does not teach a child how to plan.

It does not erase years of shame.

It does not automatically create emotional safety within a marriage.

And it cannot replace sleep, structure, therapy, connection, and consistent support.

The most effective treatment often combines several approaches according to the person's needs.

That is not weakness.

It is wisdom.

◈

THC and the ADHD Debate

This is where the conversation becomes even louder.

Cannabis use may be one of the most emotionally charged topics in discussions about ADHD treatment today.

Some people with ADHD report that THC helps them:

- slow down
- sleep
- reduce anxiety
- tolerate boredom

- manage emotional intensity
- quiet racing thoughts

Others report the opposite:

- reduced motivation
- memory difficulties
- increased anxiety
- greater avoidance
- emotional numbing
- dependence
- worsening executive dysfunction

Both experiences exist.

That is why this conversation requires honesty rather than automatic praise or condemnation.

Some people genuinely feel that cannabis helps them regulate their emotions, thoughts, or sleep.

That lived experience should not be dismissed or mocked.

But personal experience is not the same as established clinical evidence.

A 2024 position statement from the Canadian ADHD Resource Alliance cautioned against cannabis use in people with ADHD. Based on the available literature, it concluded that there was no evidence that cannabis effectively treats ADHD or improves attention and productivity. A 2023 systematic review similarly emphasized the need for further research into cannabis use, its potential benefits and risks, and its effects on ADHD symptoms and executive functioning.

That does not mean people who uses cannabis are being dishonest.

It means subjective relief does not always translate into improved functioning, and the evidence remains uncertain.

A responsible conversation must be able to hold several truths at once:

Some people report benefits.

Some experience significant harm.

Research remains limited.

Individual risk matters.

Dosage matters.

Age matters.

Frequency of use matters.

THC concentration matters.

The risk of cannabis use disorder matters.

Medical and psychiatric oversight matter.

That is not stigma.

It is clinical honesty.

◈

The Problem with Cannabis Stigma

The problem is not that clinicians raise concerns about cannabis.

They should.

Responsible care requires honest conversations about potential risks, dependence, and long-term functioning.

The problem begins when concern turns into contempt.

When someone says:

"Cannabis is the only thing that slows my brain down,"

the response should not be:

"You are just making excuses."

That response ends the conversation before anyone understands what the cannabis use is doing, why it began, or what need it may be meeting.

A more responsible response would ask:

Which symptoms does it relieve?

What does it cost you physically, emotionally, or functionally?

How often do you use it, and how much?

Does it improve your ability to function, or does it help you avoid distress temporarily?

Have you noticed changes in your memory, motivation, anxiety, sleep, or relationships?

Are there safer or more sustainable ways to address the same symptoms?

What does your treatment team recommend?

That is the difference between stigma and clinical care.

Stigma humiliates.

Clinical care investigates.

Stigma closes the conversation.

Clinical care creates space for honesty, assessment, and informed decision-making.

Stigma says:

"Bad."

Clinical care asks:

What is happening inside your nervous system, and what is this behavior helping you escape, manage, or regulate?

That shift matters.

Many people with ADHD already carry years of shame about their symptoms, coping strategies, and difficulty functioning.

When professionals respond with judgment, people learn to hide.

And when substance use becomes hidden, its risks become harder to assess, address, and treat.

◈

Psychedelics, Neuroplasticity, and Hope

Psychedelics represent another rapidly growing and deeply controversial area of mental health research.

Psilocybin.

LSD microdosing.

Ketamine.

MDMA-assisted therapy.

These conversations are now everywhere.

Some people believe psychedelic-based treatments may help address:

- trauma
- depression
- addiction
- emotional rigidity
- neuroplasticity
- self-awareness
- spiritual healing

Some people with ADHD report that microdosing improves their attention, mood, emotional regulation, or mindfulness.

A 2024 study on psychedelic microdosing and ADHD reported reductions in ADHD symptoms over time, along with increased mindfulness. However, the authors emphasized that the findings still require validation through controlled clinical trials. Another prospective study published that year described possible social and emotional benefits, but its conclusions also remained preliminary.

That is the key word:

Preliminary.

Hopeful does not mean proven.

Promising does not mean established.

Popular does not mean safe.

Illegal or unregulated use also carries serious risks.

A responsible discussion of psychedelics should not dismiss the possibility that this research may lead somewhere meaningful.

But it should not pretend the science is settled.

The most honest position is this:

Psychedelic research deserves rigorous study.

People's reported experiences deserve thoughtful attention.

But ADHD treatment should not be built on hype, social media claims, underground experimentation, or desperation alone.

Caution is especially important for people with trauma histories, bipolar-spectrum conditions or risk factors, vulnerability to psychosis, unstable substance use, or complex psychiatric needs.

Hope must be paired with caution.

That is not an anti-psychedelic position.

It is a commitment to human safety.

◈

The Danger of Misinformation

The internet has transformed the way people understand ADHD.

In some ways, beautifully.

People are finally finding language for experiences they carried in silence for years.

They are learning about:

- executive dysfunction
- emotional dysregulation
- rejection sensitivity
- masking

- burnout
- dopamine-seeking

That awareness matters.

But the internet has also unleashed an avalanche of misinformation.

Sweeping claims are repeated with absolute certainty:

- "Stimulants are always harmful."
- "THC cures ADHD."
- "Psychedelics fix executive dysfunction."
- "Medication destroys creativity."
- "Everyone with ADHD should microdose."
- "Exercise alone treats ADHD."
- "Big Pharma invented ADHD."

These claims are not merely inaccurate.

They can be dangerous.

Because desperate people listen.

Parents listen.

Teenagers listen.

People in recovery listen.

People who are frightened of medication listen.

People who have already been failed by healthcare systems listen.

And when misinformation is delivered with confidence, it can can become persuasive.

That is why conversations about ADHD treatment require literacy.

Not blind trust.

Not automatic rejection.

Literacy.

People need to ask:

- What does the research actually show?

- Who benefits from this claim?
- Is this a personal experience or clinical evidence?
- Is this safe for children or adolescents?
- Is it legal?
- Is it medically supervised?
- What are the known risks?
- What are the alternatives?
- How might my medical, psychiatric, or addiction history affect the risk?

That is how people become empowered.

Not through stigma.

Not through hype.

Through informed choice.

◈

What "Whatever Works" Really Means

When someone says, "I support people using whatever path they need," the statement can sound compassionate and empowering.

But it must be understood responsibly.

It does not mean anything goes.

It does not mean every substance is safe.

It does not mean every treatment carries the same level of evidence.

And it does not mean people should experiment without understanding the risks.

It means people deserve individualized pathways to care.

One person's healing may look very different from another's.

Treatment decisions should consider:

- symptoms
- trauma history

- addiction history
- age and developmental stage
- medical and psychiatric risks
- legal context
- current level of functioning
- family and social environment
- Culture
- access to care
- personal values

It also means clinicians should stop pretending there is only one acceptable path toward regulation and recovery.

For some people, medication changes everything.

For others, therapy becomes the turning point.

Others may build a foundation through exercise, sleep, structure, coaching, mindfulness, and consistent support.

Some people report that cannabis helps them manage certain symptoms, although the evidence remains limited and the risks require careful consideration.

Others are exploring psychedelic-assisted care, even though ADHD-specific research remains preliminary.

These options should not be treated as equally effective, equally safe, or equally well supported by evidence.

The point is not to flatten important differences between them.

The point is to stop humiliating people for seeking relief and start helping them make informed, responsible decisions.

◈

The Ethics of Treatment

A truly ethical approach to ADHD treatment must hold several truths at once:

First, ADHD is real.

Second, it can be deeply impairing.

Third, appropriate treatment can change and even save lives.

Fourth, every intervention carries potential benefits, limitations, and risks.

Ethical care therefore requires:

- informed consent
- individualized assessment
- appropriate clinical monitoring
- harm-reduction strategies
- honest discussion of benefits and risks
- respect for lived experience
- careful attention to evidence
- flexibility
- accountability

People do not need providers who shame them.

But they also do not need providers who approve every request without careful assessment.

They need professionals who can remain thoughtful in the face of uncertainty.

Who can listen without abandoning clinical judgment.

Who can acknowledge risk without using fear as a weapon.

That is where genuine clinical wisdom lives.

Not in rigid judgment. Not in reckless affirmation.

In complexity.

The Stigma That Keeps People Sick

Stigma delays treatment.

Stigma silences people.

It makes parents afraid to seek help.

It teaches adults to hide.

It pressures people in recovery to conceal the truth.

It leaves teenagers experimenting alone.

It keeps professionals from pursuing a diagnosis.

And it makes people feel broken for needing support.

Perhaps most dangerously, stigma convinces people that enduring untreated suffering is somehow more honorable than accepting help.

That belief has caused immeasurable harm.

There is nothing noble about suffering without support.

There is nothing weak about evidence-informed care.

And there is nothing shameful about needing help to regulate a nervous system.

ADHD treatment should not feel like a public trial.

It should be a private, thoughtful, informed, and humane process between the person seeking care and the qualified professionals supporting them.

Finding the Right Treatment Path

The best ADHD treatment is not the one that wins an argument online.

It is the one that helps a person function, heal, connect, regulate, and live more safely.

For one person, that may include stimulant medication.

For another, non-stimulant medication.

For someone else, therapy and coaching.

Recovery support and structure.

Trauma-informed care.

Improved sleep, exercise, and mindfulness practices.

For many people, effective treatment involves a combination of approaches.

There is no shame in needing more than one form of support.

ADHD is complex.

Its treatment may need to be complex as well.

The goal is not to make people less like themselves.

It is to help them become more fully and safely themselves.

More regulated.

More present.

More capable.

More connected.

More alive, without being consumed by internal chaos.

◈

The Real Question

The real question is not:

Are you for or against medication?

Or:

Are you for or against THC?

Or:

Are you for or against psychedelics?

Those questions reduce complex decisions to ideological positions.

The real question is:

What does this person need to build a life in which their nervous system no longer has to remain in survival mode?

That is the question beneath every treatment debate.

That is the heart of this chapter.

That is the real war over treatment.

Because when people stop defending positions long enough to listen, they often discover something painful:

Most people with ADHD are not trying to take the easy way through life.

They are trying to survive it.

Trying to focus.

Trying to sleep.

Trying to stop disappointing the people they love.

Trying to stop chasing stimulation.

Trying to stop reacting in ways they later regret.

Trying to stop numbing.

Trying to stop collapsing.

Trying to stop hating themselves.

And when a treatment helps someone move closer to dignity, stability, safety, healing, and purpose, the conversation should begin with careful assessment and respect.

Not shame.

CHAPTER ELEVEN

Burning Out

The High-Functioning Collapse of the ADHD Nervous System

◈

Running on Empty

The dangerous part was that no one knew.

No one looked at him and thought:

That man is collapsing.

From the outside, everything still looked productive.

The emails were answered.

The meetings happened.

The deadlines were met.

The social media posts still sounded motivated.

The work still got done.

People continued to praise him:

- "You are everywhere."
- "I don't know how you do it."
- "You never stop."
- "You are crushing it."

And every compliment encouraged the nervous system to remain in survival mode a little longer.

Because what no one understood was that the productivity was no longer being fueled by inspiration.

It was being driven by adrenaline, urgency, and fear of falling behind.

There is a profound difference between working from passion and functioning through chronic nervous system activation.

Many people with ADHD eventually lose sight of that difference.

The body keeps moving.

The brain keeps performing.

But beneath that performance, the nervous system begins to run out of capacity.

Sleep no longer feels restorative.

Weekends are not enough.

Even vacations may fail to help because the mind never fully leaves work behind and the body no longer remembers how to settle.

The thoughts keep moving:

- planning
- worrying
- anticipating
- replaying
- solving
- preparing
- scanning

Always scanning.

That is what many people misunderstand about ADHD burnout.

The exhaustion is not only physical.

It is cognitive.

The nervous system becomes overloaded for so long that eventually the brain itself begins losing capacity.

Simple tasks suddenly feel impossible.

Emails become overwhelming.

Phone calls feel intrusive.

Minor inconveniences trigger emotional flooding.

They begin waking up already exhausted.

Not merely tired.

Exhausted.

There is a difference.

Tiredness often improves with rest.

Burnout may not.

Because burnout is more than ordinary fatigue.

It is the nervous system signaling:

I cannot keep living at this pace.

And yet many high-functioning people with ADHD continue anyway.

Because slowing down does not feel safe.

◈

The Crash No One Saw Coming

The collapse rarely begins with a dramatic breakdown.

At first, it happens quietly.

Internally.

The person continues functioning while pieces of the nervous system begin shutting down one by one.

Concentration weakens.

Patience thins.

Emotional regulation becomes harder.

Memory grows less reliable.

Sleep becomes fragmented.

The body remains tense, even during moments that should feel restful.

But because the person is still producing, no one recognizes the warning signs.

This can be especially true for high-achieving adults with ADHD.

Professionals.

Caregivers.

Leaders.

The world often mistakes survival mode for ambition.

And that misunderstanding can quietly destroy a person.

The crash often reveals itself in ordinary moments:

Sitting in a parking lot, unable to walk into work.

Staring at an email for twenty minutes, unable to form a response.

Forgetting tasks that once felt easy.

Reacting intensely to something small.

Feeling emotionally numb while pretending to care.

Losing interest in the things that once created excitement.

By then, the mind and body may already be conserving what little energy remains.

Before a more visible breakdown, people may experience:

- emotional flatness
- panic attacks
- hopelessness
- irritability
- brain fog
- overstimulation
- task paralysis
- emotional flooding

Many people with ADHD have spent their lives learning to push through discomfort.

So they may dismiss these warning signs for months or even years.

Until the body makes ignoring them impossible.

Writers and clinicians such as Bessel van der Kolk have explored how how chronic stress and unresolved nervous system can affect the body as well as the mind.

Stress can become visible in sleep, muscle tension, pain, breathing, digestion, and the body's ability to settle.

The body continues carrying what the person has tried to outrun.

Even when the person insists they are still fine.

◈

Overcommitting to Survive

Many people with ADHD do not overcommit because they are careless.

They overcommit because stimulation can temporarily make the nervous system feel more organized.

Busy feels productive.

Busy feels valuable.

Busy keeps the mind occupied.

Busy can prevent painful emotions from becoming loud enough to hear.

Over time, this creates a dangerous relationship with overcommitment.

The person says yes to:

- too many projects
- too many responsibilities

- too many obligations
- too many people's emotional needs

Because stopping creates stillness.

And in that stillness, everything they have been outrunning may begin to surface:

- shame
- grief
- loneliness
- exhaustion
- anxiety

So they keep moving.

They begin depending on:

- urgency
- deadlines
- multitasking
- pressure
- adrenaline

Not because they enjoy suffering.

Because intensity has become familiar.

For some people with ADHD, chaos can feel safer than peace.

Chaos feels active.

Predictable.

Alive.

Peace feels unfamiliar.

Exposed.

Sometimes even threatening.

Over time, that conditioning becomes destructive.

Modern culture often reinforces it.

People applaud:

- overworking

- sleeping less
- constant availability
- nonstop productivity

Many people with ADHD are especially vulnerable to that praise because they have spent years trying to prove:

I am not lazy.

That fear becomes fuel.

They overextend themselves, trying desperately to outrun shame.

They keep saying yes.

Keep performing.

Keep carrying more than one nervous system was ever meant to hold.

Until the body can no longer sustain the pace.

And the life that looked impressive from the outside begins collapsing from within.

◈

The Exhausted High Achiever

Some of the most burned-out people are still remarkably successful on the outside.

That contradiction lies at the heart of high-functioning ADHD burnout.

The outside world sees:

- achievement
- leadership
- charisma
- intelligence
- productivity

Inside, the person may be experiencing:

- emotional flooding
- panic
- numbness
- exhaustion
- overstimulation
- hopelessness

Many high-functioning people with ADHD become skilled at masking how much they are struggling.

Professionals.

Clinicians.

Educators.

Entrepreneurs.

People working in recovery services and other helping professions.

Helping others can provide stimulation, purpose, urgency, emotional connection, and an immediate sense of usefulness.

In a crisis, a person with ADHD may appear exceptionally capable.

The urgency sharpens attention.

The pressure creates momentum.

The need feels clear.

That competence can create the illusion that everything is under control.

Eventually, the nervous system paying the price for years of operating under chronic pressure.

And the frightening part is this:

Many high-functioning people continue performing while privately fantasizing about disappearing completely from every responsibility they carry.

Not necessarily from life.

From the pressure.

The expectations.

The endless need to be available.

They long for escape.

Silence.

Rest.

Stillness.

Anything that would allow the nervous system to finally carrying so much for a little while.

That level of exhaustion can become profoundly isolating because the people around them keep saying:

"You are doing amazing."

Meanwhile, behind the performance, the person feels as though they are quietly drowning.

◈

When the Body Finally Says No

Eventually, the body demands attention.

No one can function in a prolonged state of survival indefinitely without consequences.

The warning signs grow louder:

- chest tightness
- panic attacks
- headaches
- insomnia
- digestive problems
- emotional volatility
- brain fog
- chronic fatigue
- physical pain

- emotional numbness

The body begins expressing what the mind has spent years trying to avid.

Many people with ADHD push past exhaustion through:

- caffeine
- adrenaline
- hyperfocus
- overworking
- substance use
- constant urgency

These strategies may keep them functioning temporarily.

But eventually, compensation stops working.

That moment can be terrifying.

Especially for high achievers.

Their identity may have become inseparable from performance.

They no longer know who they are without productivity.

So when the body finally says:

No more.

the collapse may feel larger than physical exhaustion.

It can become a crisis of identity.

Questions begin to surface:

- Who am I if I stop producing?
- Who am I if I cannot perform?
- Who am I when I rest?
- Am I still valuable if I slow down?

These questions reveal how deeply productivity culture can shape a person's sense of worth.

For people with ADHD who already carry years of shame, slowing down may feel like proof of every accusation they have spent their lives trying to outrun.

Lazy.

Unreliable.

Undisciplined.

Not enough.

The body may be asking for rest.

But shame interprets rest as failure.

◈

Rest Feels Unsafe

One of the saddest realities of ADHD burnout is that many people no longer know how to rest.

Not deeply.

Not without guilt.

Not without searching for something else to do.

The body may stop moving.

But the mind continues running.

Thoughts race.

Plans form.

Anxiety searches for somewhere to go.

Even in a quiet room, the person remains internally alert.

For many people with ADHD, stillness can feel deeply uncomfortable because it removes distraction.

And when distraction disappears, the emotions buried beneath constant activity may begin to surface:

- shame
- grief
- regret
- loneliness
- trauma
- exhaustion

This is one reason some people remain almost constantly overstimulated.

Scrolling.

Working.

Talking.

Planning.

Creating.

Helping.

Moving.

Anything except silence.

Because silence can bring them face-to-face with everything they have been trying not to feel.

That realization can be heartbreaking.

Especially for adults who have spent decades surviving through motion.

Their nervous system may have learned:

If I stop moving, everything will catch up with me.

So even rest can trigger anxiety.

Recovering from burnout may require learning something many people with ADHD were never taught:

You are safe even when you are not performing.

You still matter when you are not producing.

That lesson becomes life-changing.

◈

Learning to Slow Down

Learning to slow down is not laziness.

For many people with ADHD, it becomes neurological rehabilitation.

After years of chronic activation, balance may no longer feel natural.

The person may understand only:

- urgency
- overstimulation
- pressure
- productivity
- chaos

Calm can feel unfamiliar.

Rest can feel undeserved.

A slower pace can feel like failure.

Healing therefore requires rebuilding a sense of safety, one practice at a time:

- sleep
- clearer boundaries
- therapy
- exercise
- structure
- emotional regulation skills
- mindfulness
- reduced overstimulation
- intentional rest
- safe, supportive relationships
- recovery support
- purpose that does not demand self-destruction

Eventually, many people with ADHD confront a painful truth:

The same intensity that helped them build remarkable lives may also have brought them dangerously close to physical and emotional collapse.

That recognition can change their priorities.

Because at some point, staying well becomes more important than appearing unstoppable.

They begin to understand:

- peace matters.
- rest matters.
- nervous system regulation matters
- emotional safety matters.

And perhaps most importantly, their worth was never meant to depend entirely on how much they could produce.

That truth can be difficult to accept.

Especially for high achievers.

Especially for people who have been praised for overperforming while their suffering went unnoticed.

But healing often begins when they finally allow themselves to hear:

You do not have to destroy yourself to prove that you matter.

For many people with ADHD, that may be one of the most important lessons of all.

PART IV

ADHD IN THE MODERN WORLD

CHAPTER TWELVE

The Kids We Keep Misunderstanding

ADHD in Children, Parenting, School Systems, Shame, and Raising an Electric Mind

◈

The Child Who Couldn't Sit Still

I was not trying to be bad.

That is the first thing adults need to understand.

I was not sitting in that classroom planning how to ruin the day. I was not trying to frustrate my teacher, embarrass my parents, interrupt the lesson, or make everyone look at me again.

That was never what was happening.

What was happening was much harder for a child to explain.

My body felt as if it carried more electricity than it could contain.

My thoughts moved faster than the lesson.

My emotions arrived before I had the language to name them or the skills to manage them.

So when adults told me to calm down, sit still, stop talking, pay attention, relax, focus, behave, or "just listen," I wanted to obey.

I really did.

But something inside me kept moving faster than my intentions.

I remember sitting in class and trying so hard to be good that it almost hurt.

My legs bounced beneath the desk.

I pressed my feet hard into the floor.

I locked my hands together.

Inside my head, I repeated the same desperate instructions:

Don't move.

Don't talk.

Don't interrupt.

Don't get in trouble again.

Then something would pull me away.

A sound outside the window.

A pencil hitting the floor.

A thought that felt too urgent to wait.

A joke that reached my mouth before my self-control could catch it.

A feeling that grew too large, too quickly.

Then suddenly, the teacher's voice would cut through the room.

"Joseph."

That was all it took.

One word. My name.

The whole class seemed to turn toward me.

My face burned.

My stomach tightened.

My heart started beating harder.

And before anyone said anything else, the shame was already there.

I did it again.

Why can't I stop?

Why does everyone else know how to be normal?

That is what many children with ADHD carry quietly.

Not only hyperactivity.

Not only distraction.

Shame.

A child with ADHD may look defiant while feeling deeply embarrassed.

They may seem careless while caring so much that every correction feels like another wound.

They may appear distracted when their nervous system is actually overwhelmed by too much sound, movement, pressure, and emotion at once.

Adults often see the behavior first.

But they do not always see the battle underneath it.

They do not see the child trying.

They do not see the shame forming.

They do not see how many times that child has already whispered, *"Please don't mess this up again."*

And this is where the damage begins.

Because when a child is misunderstood long enough, they may stop thinking, *"I am struggling."*

They may begin believing, *"I am bad."*

One of the most painful parts of ADHD is not the diagnosis itself.

It is the shame that grows around it when a child's pain is mistaken for disobedience.

◈

Boys, Girls, and Missed Diagnoses

For generations, the public image of ADHD was painfully narrow.

A young boy.

Loud.

Hyperactive.

Disruptive.

Unable to sit still.

That image was not entirely wrong.

But it was incomplete.

And because it was incomplete, countless children went unnoticed.

Especially girls.

Quiet children.

Gifted children.

Anxious children.

Children who learned to mask their struggles.

Boys with ADHD are often more likely to be noticed when their symptoms are visible. They may appear physically restless, impulsive, hyperactive, or disruptive in the classroom. They may interrupt, blurt out answers, leave their seats, or struggle to meet behavioral expectations.

Those boys are often identified early.

Sometimes accurately.

Sometimes harshly.

Sometimes both.

But many girls with ADHD are misunderstood in different ways.

Their symptoms may be internalized, masked, or mistaken for something else.

Instead of moving constantly around the room, they may appear:

- anxious
- daydreamy
- emotionally sensitive

- overwhelmed
- disorganized
- perfectionistic
- socially exhausted
- forgetful
- quietly distressed

They may not disrupt the room.

So the room may fail to notice them.

That can be devastating.

Because suffering that does not inconvenience adults is often easier to overlook.

A girl may sit silently in class while her thoughts race.

She may spend hours completing homework because organizing her ideas and beginning each task feel overwhelming.

She may cry in private because she believes she is lazy, stupid, or falling behind.

She may become a people-pleaser because rejection feels unbearable.

She may rely on perfectionism because making a mistake feels emotionally unsafe.

And the adults around her may say:

"She's just anxious."

"She's dramatic."

"She is too sensitive."

"She needs more confidence."

"She's smart, but she needs to apply herself."

Meanwhile, the ADHD remains hidden beneath the mask.

This matters because a missed or delayed diagnosis can shape the course of a child's life.

Children whose struggles remain misunderstood may develop additional wounds:

- anxiety
- depression
- chronic shame
- low self-esteem
- school avoidance
- social insecurity
- emotional dysregulation
- increased vulnerability to addiction later in life

The earlier a child is understood accurately, the sooner adults can respond with compassion, structure, and appropriate support instead of criticism.

But accurate understanding requires adults to look beyond familiar stereotypes.

ADHD does not have a single appearance.

It can look loud.

It can look quiet.

It can look angry.

It can look anxious.

It can look gifted.

It can look disorganized.

It can look like perfectionism.

It can look like emotional outbursts.

It can look like a child who appears composed throughout the school day, then falls apart the moment they arrive home because they have spent hours suppressing their needs and holding themselves together.

Parents and educators need to understand this:

A child does not have to disrupt a room to be struggling inside it.

School Trauma

School can become one of the first places where children with ADHD learn shame.

Not because teachers are bad people.

Many teachers care deeply.

Many are overwhelmed themselves.

They are trying to manage large classes, limited resources, behavioral needs, administrative pressure, and expectations that can feel impossible to meet.

But when school systems do not understand ADHD, children suffer.

A child with ADHD may spend six or seven hours each day in an environment that requires:

- sitting still
- waiting for their turn
- sustaining attention
- staying organized
- using working memory
- regulating emotions
- controlling impulses
- managing time
- completing tasks

In other words, school demands many of the very skills ADHD can make difficult.

Then, when the child struggles, they may be punished for the symptoms they have not yet learned to manage.

That is the tragedy.

The child forgets their homework.

Loses important papers.

Blurts out an answer.

Moves too much.

Stares out the window.

Has an emotional meltdown.

Avoids a difficult task.

Becomes frustrated.

Instead of asking, *"What skill is missing?"* adults often ask, *"Why won't this child behave?"*

One question leads toward punishment.

The other opens the door to support.

What is this child struggling to regulate, understand, or communicate?

That question can change everything.

School trauma does not always begin with one catastrophic event.

Sometimes, it develops through repetition.

Repeated embarrassment.

Repeated correction.

Repeated public discipline.

Repeated report-card comments.

Repeated disappointment.

Repeated social rejection.

Repeated messages that the child is not trying hard enough.

Over time, the child may begin to associate school with emotional danger.

Not curiosity.

Not discovery.

Danger.

The body remembers:

- the teacher's tone
- the sound of the class laughing

- the missing assignment
- the failed test
- the red marks across the page
- the conversation in the hallway
- the feeling of being different

Many adults with ADHD still carry these school wounds decades later.

They remember being called lazy.

Being humiliated in front of others.

Being told they had potential, usually followed by a reminder that they were wasting it.

They remember feeling unintelligent even when they knew they were capable.

That is why schools must move away from punishment-based responses and toward support-based care.

A child with ADHD does not need adults to lower expectations.

They need adults to provide a different pathway toward meeting them.

That may include:

- clear structure
- visual supports
- movement breaks
- concise instructions
- reduced shame
- emotional regulation skills
- Executive functioning support
- positive reinforcement
- predictability
- compassion
- accountability without humiliation

Children with ADHD can succeed.

But success becomes far more difficult in environments that mistake dysregulation for defiance and unmet needs for bad behavior.

◈

The Medication Debate

Few topics cause parents more fear than ADHD medication.

That fear is understandable.

Parents wonder:

- Will medication change my child?
- Will my child become dependent on it?
- Will it affect their personality?
- Are we taking the easy way out?
- What will other people think?
- Are we failing as parents?

These are deeply human questions.

But fear should not be the only voice in the room.

Medication is not a moral failure.

It is not a parenting failure.

And it is not proof that a child is broken.

For many children, appropriately prescribed ADHD medication can be life-changing.

It may support:

- attention
- impulse control
- emotional regulation
- task completion
- frustration tolerance
- classroom functioning

- safety
- confidence

For some children, medication provides enough neurological support for them to use the skills adults are trying to teach.

That does not mean medication is always necessary.

Nor does it mean medication is perfect or that every child will respond in the same way.

Parents should still pay close attention to side effects and other concerns.

It means medication deserves thoughtful, informed, and individualized consideration.

Not stigma.

Not fear.

Not internet panic.

Not shame.

Some children benefit from stimulant medication.

Others benefit from non-stimulant medication.

Some need therapy.

Some need parent training.

Some need school accommodations.

Some need sleep support.

Some need occupational therapy.

Some need trauma-informed care.

Many need a combination of these supports.

The best treatment plan is not the one that wins an argument online.

It is the one that helps a child function, learn, regulate emotions, connect with others, and feel less ashamed.

Parents also need to understand this:

Untreated ADHD carries risks, too.

Without adequate support, ADHD can contribute to:

- academic difficulties
- low self-esteem
- anxiety
- depression
- impulsive risk-taking
- social struggles
- family conflict
- greater vulnerability to addiction later in life

The decision is not simply between "medication" and "nothing."

It is about determining what kind of support this particular child needs.

That decision should be made carefully, with input from qualified professionals, the family, and, when appropriate, the child.

Children deserve treatment plans built around dignity, not fear.

◈

What Parents Need to Understand

Parents need to understand that ADHD is not a character flaw.

It is not the result of bad parenting.

It is not a lack of discipline.

It is not a child choosing to be difficult.

ADHD is a neurodevelopmental disorder that affects multiple forms of self-regulation.

This means a child may struggle with:

- regulating attention
- regulating emotions
- controlling impulses
- sustaining motivation
- managing time

- starting and completing tasks
- processing sensory input

A child may know what to do and still struggle to do it.

That is one of the hardest realities for parents to accept.

From the outside, ADHD can look like a choice.

The child knows they have homework.

But they do not start.

The child knows they should not interrupt.

But they blurt out.

The child knows the routine.

But they forget.

The child knows they should calm down.

But their emotions continue to escalate.

Parents often say:

"They know better."

And that may be true.

But knowing what to do is not the same as being able to regulate consistently enough to do it.

That understanding creates a central shift in parenting.

From:

"My child won't."

To:

"My child is struggling to."

This shift does not remove accountability.

It changes how accountability is taught.

Children with ADHD still need limits.

They still need structure.

They still need clear expectations.

They still need appropriate consequences.

But they need these things delivered without shame.

A child can be corrected without being humiliated.

A child can be held accountable without being emotionally crushed.

A child can be taught skills without being labeled lazy, dramatic, or bad.

Parents must learn to separate the child from the behavior.

The behavior may require intervention.

The child still needs connection.

That distinction matters.

Connection is not a reward given only after a child learns to regulate.

Connection is often what makes regulation possible.

◈

Raising an Electric Mind

Raising a child with ADHD requires a different kind of parenting.

Not permissive parenting.

Not harsh parenting.

Regulated parenting.

A child with an electric mind needs adults who can serve as emotional anchors.

That does not mean parents must be perfect.

No parent is.

But children with ADHD often rely on the adults around them for co-regulation.

When the adult escalates, the child's nervous system may escalate further.

When the adult responds with shame, the child may begin to internalize that shame.

When the adult remains calm, firm, and connected, the child has a better chance of learning how to regulate over time.

This is difficult.

Especially when the parent is exhausted.

Especially when the parent also has ADHD.

Especially when the child's behavior awakens the parent's own childhood wounds.

Many parents raising children with ADHD are also living with ADHD themselves.

They may be trying to help a child regulate while still learning how to regulate their own emotions, impulses, and responses.

That is hard.

Those parents need compassion, too.

They need support.

They need education.

They need breaks.

They need practical tools.

They need to understand their child without carrying the weight of constant self-blame.

Raising an electric mind means learning to ask better questions:

- What overstimulates this child?
- What helps this child reset?
- What time of day is most difficult?
- Which transitions tend to trigger dysregulation?
- How does hunger affect their behavior?
- How does sleep affect their emotional regulation?
- Which environments overwhelm them?
- What strengths make them feel engaged and alive?
- What kind of structure supports them without crushing their spirit?
- What kind of praise genuinely builds their confidence?

Parents must become investigators, not prosecutors.

Behavior is often a form of communication.

Meltdowns may communicate overwhelm.

Avoidance may communicate fear, anxiety, or executive dysfunction.

Defiance may communicate frustration or a need for control.

Impulsivity may reflect difficulty with inhibition.

Clinginess may communicate anxiety or insecurity.

Anger may be protecting a deeper sense of shame.

The goal is not to excuse every behavior.

The goal is to understand the need or function beneath it.

That is where meaningful change begins.

◈

Protecting Children From Shame

If there is one message every parent, teacher, coach, therapist, and family member needs to understand, it is this:

Children with ADHD do not need more shame.

Most already carry far too much of it.

They need:

- structure without humiliation
- accountability without rejection
- correction without cruelty
- support without pity
- belief in their potential without denial of their struggles
- advocacy without enabling harmful behavior

Shame does not make children with ADHD stronger.

Shame teaches them to hide.

Shame teaches them to lie to avoid punishment or disappointment.

Shame teaches them to withdraw from challenges.

Shame teaches them to overcompensate in an effort to prove their worth.

Over time, shame can teach them to hate themselves.

Eventually, that shame may contribute to anxiety, depression, substance misuse, and emotional collapse.

Protecting children from shame does not mean protecting them from consequences.

It means making consequences instructive rather than damaging to their identity.

A child should never walk away from correction believing:

"I am bad."

They should walk away understanding:

"That behavior needs to change, but I am still loved."

That distinction can shape the course of a child's life.

Children with ADHD need adults who see beyond the disruption.

They need adults who recognize:

- the creativity
- the sensitivity
- the humor
- the intelligence
- the emotional depth
- the potential
- the pain beneath the behavior

The child who cannot sit still may one day be the person who changes the energy of an entire room.

The child who talks too much may become a speaker whose words save lives.

The child who feels deeply may become a healer.

The child who questions everything may become an innovator.

The child who struggles within rigid systems may grow up to build better ones.

But first, that child must make it through childhood without learning to believe they are broken.

That is the responsibility of the adults around them.

Not to make electric children smaller.

But to help them understand, direct, and carry their electricity safely.

CHAPTER THIRTEEN

Masking the Chaos

ADHD in Women, Misdiagnosis, Emotional Suppression, Trauma, and the Exhaustion of Pretending

◈

The Performance of Normal

If you met her at work, you might never know.

That was what made the mask so dangerous.

She arrived early.

She always looked put together.

She answered emails.

She helped everyone.

She smiled constantly.

She remembered birthdays.

She handled one crisis after another.

People described her as:

- dependable
- professional
- caring
- organized
- strong

Yet every night, she went home and quietly fell apart.

No one saw the panic attacks in the bathroom.

No one saw the overstimulation.

No one saw the emotional exhaustion that came from masking her symptoms all day.

No one saw the laundry piled in corners because, after performing "normal" for twelve straight hours, her nervous system had nothing left to give.

No one saw the missed appointments concealed beneath layers of phone reminders, alarms, and frantic self-correction.

No one saw her replaying every social interaction at two o'clock in the morning, wondering:

"Did I say too much?"

"Did they think I was weird?"

"Why can't I stop overthinking everything?"

No one saw how overwhelmed her nervous system was beneath the performance.

This is what many women with ADHD become experts at:

appearing functional while privately falling apart.

Because they can become so skilled at masking, they may go decades without understanding what is happening in their brains and nervous systems.

Instead, they are labeled:

- anxious
- dramatic
- emotional
- lazy
- disorganized
- "too sensitive"
- "too intense"

- "too much"

Or worse:

they begin to label themselves the same way.

This is the tragedy of masked ADHD.

The suffering remains invisible.

Especially in women.

Especially intelligent women.

Especially outwardly capable women whose competence conceals how much they are struggling.

Especially women raised in environments where accommodating other people's emotions became a means of survival.

Many girls learn early:

Being liked matters.

Being agreeable matters.

Being emotionally manageable matters.

So they adapt.

They suppress.

They overperform.

They people-please.

Eventually, they grow exhausted from trying to survive inside an identity built around hiding how their nervous system actually works.

◈

ADHD in Women

For years, much of ADHD research and public attention centered on hyperactive young boys.

That focus powerfully shaped public understanding.

The stereotype became:

- loud
- impulsive

- disruptive
- physically hyperactive

But many women with ADHD do not appear that way outwardly.

Their symptoms may be:

- internalized
- emotionally masked
- socially compensated for
- obscured by anxiety or perfectionism

Many women with ADHD become chronic overthinkers.

Not because they are weak.

But because their minds and nervous systems may feel as though they never stop processing.

Many struggle with:

- racing thoughts
- emotional overwhelm
- sensory overload
- chronic shame
- executive dysfunction
- people-pleasing
- rejection sensitivity
- emotional exhaustion

Yet because they continue to function outwardly, few people recognize the neurological and emotional overload occurring in private.

Researchers and clinicians, including Sari Solden, have written extensively about how ADHD in women may be misunderstood, minimized, or missed because of masking, internalized symptoms, and social conditioning.

Many women spend years believing:

"Something is wrong with me."

Not because they lack intelligence.

But because they cannot understand why ordinary life feels so overwhelming.

Why simple tasks feel impossible on some days.

Why emotional regulation requires so much effort.

Why overstimulation feels unbearable.

Why their minds and bodies rarely seem to fully relax.

Because many women become socially skilled at compensating, their struggles may remain hidden until they experience:

- burnout
- emotional collapse
- anxiety disorders
- depression
- relationship breakdown
- addiction
- profound exhaustion or shutdown

Only then do many women finally receive answers.

For some, the diagnosis itself can feel emotionally overwhelming because decades of confusion suddenly begin to make sense.

◈

When ADHD Looks Like Anxiety

Many women with ADHD are diagnosed with anxiety long before ADHD is considered.

Sometimes both conditions are present.

They may also overlap significantly.

But many women describe spending years receiving treatment for anxiety while underlying difficulties with executive functioning and emotional regulation went unrecognized.

And honestly?

That pattern is understandable.

ADHD-related difficulties can generate repeated anxiety.

Imagine moving through each day:

- forgetting things
- losing things
- falling behind
- masking symptoms
- overthinking conversations
- becoming emotionally flooded
- fearing rejection
- struggling to organize daily life

Of course, anxiety can develop.

The nervous system may rarely feel settled or safe.

Many women become hypervigilant because they are constantly trying to compensate for their symptoms in private.

They double-check everything.

They overprepare.

They monitor themselves in social situations.

They work desperately to avoid mistakes.

That level of self-monitoring becomes psychologically exhausting.

And because many women are socialized to preserve harmony and maintain emotional control, they may internalize distress instead of expressing it outwardly.

The result?

A woman may appear:

- anxious
- perfectionistic
- emotionally overwhelmed

- chronically stressed

while ADHD remains hidden beneath the surface.

Over time, that hidden suffering can become devastating.

Especially when women interpret their struggles as moral failures rather than neurological differences.

◈

The BPD Overlap

Few conversations create more confusion, stigma, and emotional intensity than the overlap between ADHD and borderline personality disorder, or BPD.

This chapter matters deeply because many people, especially women, have spent years being misunderstood within this overlap.

To have an honest conversation, both conditions must be approached with compassion rather than judgment.

There are real areas of overlap between ADHD and BPD, including:

- emotional dysregulation
- impulsivity
- rejection sensitivity
- intense relationships
- mood instability
- emotional flooding
- anger
- identity struggles

From the outside, some behaviors can appear remarkably similar.

But similarity does not mean sameness.

Unfortunately, many women with ADHD have historically been:

- misdiagnosed

- dismissed
- stigmatized
- invalidated

This is especially true when emotional intensity becomes visible in clinical settings.

Some women genuinely have both ADHD and BPD.

Some have ADHD with trauma-related emotional dysregulation.

Some have complex PTSD that may be misinterpreted as personality pathology.

Some experience chronic rejection sensitivity that can create emotional instability resembling BPD from the outside.

This is why nuanced clinical assessment matters enormously.

Labels shape identity.

When emotionally dysregulated women are labeled carelessly, without careful attention to the underlying nervous system, trauma history, and developmental context, serious psychological harm can occur.

Researchers continue to explore the connections among ADHD, trauma, emotional dysregulation, attachment disruption, and personality-related diagnoses.

The goal is not to erase meaningful distinctions between diagnoses.

The goal is this:

people deserve careful understanding before they are reduced to labels.

Especially emotionally overwhelmed women who have spent years surviving through masking and self-suppression.

◈

Trauma, Shame, and Masking

Many women with ADHD carry not only neurological dysregulation, but also chronic shame layered on top of it.

This is especially true for women raised in environments where:

- emotional sensitivity was criticized
- perfectionism was rewarded
- mistakes were punished
- people-pleasing became a form of survival
- conflict felt unsafe

Many girls learn:

- Don't be loud
- Don't be difficult
- Don't be emotional
- Don't inconvenience people
- Don't fail publicly

So they begin performing regulation instead of actually experiencing it internally.

That performance becomes masking.

And masking becomes exhausting.

Beneath the polished exterior, the nervous system may still feel:

- chaotic
- overstimulated
- emotionally flooded
- deeply anxious
- ashamed
- exhausted

Over time, many women become disconnected from themselves.

They become experts at becoming who everyone else needs them to be.

Helpful.

Reliable.

Pleasant.

Accommodating.

Emotionally available.

Meanwhile, in private, they may think:

"I don't even know who I am anymore."

That disconnection from identity can become deeply painful.

Especially because many women with masked ADHD are praised for the very coping mechanisms that are quietly destroying them inside.

◈

The Exhaustion of Pretending

Masking consumes enormous emotional energy.

It is the constant self-monitoring.

The overthinking.

The emotional suppression.

The hyperawareness.

The daily performance of appearing "normal."

Over time, the nervous system grows exhausted from pretending. Many women reach a point where they can no longer sustain the performance mentally or emotionally. What looks like a sudden collapse from the outside is often the visible result of years of silent strain.

That collapse may appear as:

- burnout
- panic attacks

- depression
- emotional numbness
- rage
- withdrawal
- nervous system shutdown

Because many masked women have spent years being the dependable one, the one who keeps functioning, people around them are often shocked when the collapse finally becomes visible.

But the collapse was never sudden.

It had been building quietly for years.

This is why diagnosis later in life can feel profoundly emotional. Many women describe grief after diagnosis, not because ADHD means hopelessness, but because they begin to understand how long they suffered without knowing why.

They begin reprocessing:

- childhood
- school
- relationships
- self-worth
- emotional struggles

through an entirely different lens.

And often, the first emotion is not relief.

It is grief.

Grief for the younger version of themselves who believed they were broken.

◈

Learning to Exist Authentically

For many women with ADHD, healing begins the moment they stop trying to become emotionally acceptable at the cost of themselves.

That does not mean abandoning accountability.

It means abandoning shame-based performance.

It means learning:

- nervous system regulation
- boundaries
- emotional honesty
- self-compassion
- sensory awareness
- authentic communication
- realistic expectations

It means recognizing this truth:

"I am not failing because I struggle differently."

Many women with ADHD have spent their lives trying to survive in systems that were never designed for their nervous systems. And despite the exhaustion, many became:

- deeply empathetic
- intuitive
- creative
- emotionally intelligent
- resilient
- extraordinary caretakers
- visionary leaders

Not because the suffering was good.

But because surviving invisible chaos often sharpens emotional perception in profound ways.

Still, survival should not require self-erasure.

Perhaps that is the most important message in this entire chapter:

Women with ADHD do not need to become less emotional, less intense, or less themselves to deserve peace.

They deserve environments where they no longer have to perform normalcy just to feel worthy of love, understanding, and rest.

Because behind countless "high-functioning" women quietly drowning inside is often the same heartbreaking truth:

They were never weak.

They were exhausted from pretending they were okay.

CHAPTER FOURTEEN

Scrolling Ourselves Sick

Social Media, Dopamine Overload, Validation Seeking, and the ADHD Nervous System in the Digital Age

◈

The Infinite Scroll

It started with one video.

That was all.

Just one quick scroll before bed.

One quick check of notifications.

One quick dopamine hit.

Then suddenly, it was two o'clock in the morning.

Again.

The room was dark, except for the blue light reflecting off his face.

His thumb kept moving on its own.

Scroll.

Laugh.

Scroll.

Shock.

Scroll.

Validation.

Scroll.

Anger.

Scroll.

Dopamine.

Scroll.

Comparison.

Scroll.

Stimulation.

His body was exhausted.

His nervous system was not.

And somewhere deep in the brain, something whispered:

"Just one more."

That sentence has become one of the defining psychological loops of the digital age for many people with ADHD.

Just one more video.

Just one more refresh.

Just one more notification.

Just one more hit of stimulation before trying to settle down.

But the nervous system does not settle.

It accelerates.

That is the tragedy of the modern attention economy.

The world has learned how to profit from dysregulated attention.

And ADHD nervous systems can be especially vulnerable.

Apps are not designed primarily to protect happiness.

They are designed to capture attention.

ADHD brains may be especially susceptible because ADHD involves differences in:

- dopamine regulation
- novelty-seeking
- impulsivity

- reward processing
- stimulation needs

Social media platforms have learned how to exploit many of these vulnerabilities.

The result?

Many people now live in a state of near-constant overstimulation.

And many do not realize how neurologically overwhelmed they have become.

◈

Dopamine on Demand

The ADHD nervous system often craves stimulation.

That is not weakness.

It is neuroscience.

Dopamine plays major roles in:

- motivation
- reward
- anticipation
- novelty
- engagement
- attention

Social media delivers stimulation rapidly.

Fast videos.

Bright colors.

Emotional content.

Instant novelty.

Endless unpredictability.

The nervous system struggles to settle because the brain keeps anticipating:

"Maybe the next scroll will feel even better."

That unpredictability can become neurologically compelling.

Not because people are morally weak.

But because variable reward systems are psychologically powerful.

The same reinforcement mechanisms involved in gambling can also appear in many forms of digital engagement.

Notifications become small reward cues.

Likes become validation cues.

Comments become emotional reinforcement.

Outrage becomes stimulation.

Conflict becomes stimulation.

Even doomscrolling becomes stimulation.

That is why many people with ADHD may feel simultaneously:

- overstimulated
- emotionally exhausted
- unable to stop scrolling

The nervous system becomes trapped between depletion and craving.

Unfortunately, much of modern technology is designed to exploit that cycle.

◈

TikTok, ADHD, and Mental Health

Few platforms have shaped ADHD culture as powerfully as TikTok.

For many people, TikTok became the first place they ever encountered words like:

- executive dysfunction
- masking
- rejection sensitivity
- hyperfocus

- emotional dysregulation

And honestly?

That matters.

For countless adults, social media offered validation they had never received from:

- schools
- parents
- clinicians
- relationships
- society

People suddenly realized:

"Wait. Other people feel this too?"

That emotional recognition changed lives.

Especially for adults who spent decades believing they were:

- lazy
- broken
- dramatic
- failing
- emotionally defective

Social media helped many people finally find language for their nervous system experiences.

That is powerful.

But there is another side to this conversation.

The same platforms that create awareness can also create overstimulation, misinformation, comparison, emotional flooding, shortened attention spans, and identity confusion.

ADHD content online often exists between two extremes:

- deeply validating and educational
- dangerously oversimplified and performative

Some creators educate responsibly.

Others reduce complex neurodevelopmental conditions to aesthetic personality traits.

That distinction matters enormously.

ADHD is not simply:

- forgetting keys
- talking fast
- being quirky
- loving iced coffee
- multitasking badly

ADHD can involve:

- severe emotional dysregulation
- addiction vulnerability
- burnout
- profound exhaustion or shutdown
- executive dysfunction
- chronic shame
- suicidality
- relationship instability

Reducing ADHD to entertainment alone minimizes real suffering.

At the same time, dismissing online ADHD communities with shame or mockery also causes harm.

The truth lives somewhere in the middle.

Social media has helped millions feel seen.

It has also pushed many people toward deeper overstimulation and emotional exhaustion.

Both things are true.

The Attention Economy

Modern technology is not neutral.

That is one of the most important truths people need to understand.

Many digital platforms are designed to keep attention captured and nervous systems activated for as long as possible.

Every:

- notification
- vibration
- refresh
- autoplay feature
- recommendation algorithm
- streak
- infinite scroll feature

is shaped by engagement psychology.

The longer a platform holds attention, the more valuable that attention becomes.

For people with ADHD, this can be especially difficult because novelty itself can feel neurologically rewarding.

The brain keeps chasing:

- stimulation
- surprise
- validation
- urgency
- emotional activation

Over time, this can create profound psychological consequences.

People may begin to struggle with:

- sustained attention

- boredom tolerance
- emotional regulation
- patience
- delayed gratification
- nervous system stillness

The brain adapts to constant stimulation.

Then ordinary life begins to feel emotionally insufficient by comparison.

Conversations feel slower.

Books feel harder.

Silence feels uncomfortable.

Stillness feels unbearable.

The nervous system becomes conditioned to expect constant activation.

Eventually, many people begin to mistake overstimulation for normal functioning.

◈

Validation Seeking

One of the deepest psychological traps of social media involves validation.

Humans are wired for social connection.

For approval.

For belonging.

For recognition.

Social media has transformed those emotional needs into visible, measurable metrics:

- likes
- shares
- followers

- comments
- views

That visibility can affect the nervous system profoundly.

This is especially true for people with ADHD, whose nervous systems may already be more sensitive to rejection, reward, dopamine-seeking and emotional feedback.

The brain begins to associate self-worth with engagement.

A person posts something.

Then waits.

Checks.

Refreshes.

Checks again.

The nervous system becomes emotionally attached to the response.

Because online validation is unpredictable, the reinforcement can become even stronger.

This can create harmful emotional cycles:

- comparison
- insecurity
- performance-based identity
- emotional dependency
- chronic self-monitoring

Many people stop asking:

"Do I like myself?"

and begin asking:

"Are people responding to me?"

That shift can become psychologically devastating.

Especially for younger generations growing up inside digital validation systems before they have fully developed a stable sense of self.

The Nervous System Was Never Built for This

Human nervous systems evolved slowly.

Modern technology accelerated rapidly.

The brain was never designed to process:

- thousands of emotional inputs each day
- nonstop notifications
- constant comparison
- global outrage cycles
- algorithmic stimulation
- 24-hour accessibility
- infinite entertainment

This is especially difficult for ADHD nervous systems that may already struggle with regulation.

Many people now live in a state of near-constant, low-level nervous system activation.

Always reachable.

Always stimulated.

Always processing.

Always consuming.

Always reacting.

And because overstimulation has become culturally normalized, many people fail to recognize how dysregulated they feel physically and emotionally.

The nervous system rarely fully rests.

Even at night.

People fall asleep holding their phones.

Wake up checking their phones.

Eat while scrolling.

Drive while distracted.

Watch television while consuming social media at the same time.

The brain rarely experiences uninterrupted stillness anymore.

Over time, that constant fragmentation can weaken the capacity for sustained attention.

For people with ADHD who already struggle with executive functioning, the impact can be profound.

◈

When the Internet Becomes Escape

For many people with ADHD, social media becomes an emotional escape.

Not because they are shallow.

But because scrolling temporarily distracts them from:

- shame
- loneliness
- anxiety
- boredom
- emotional pain
- overwhelm

The brain receives rapid stimulation without requiring emotional vulnerability.

That can become deeply compelling.

Especially during burnout.

Especially during depression.

Especially during emotional dysregulation.

A person may spend hours online not because they are truly enjoying themselves, but because they are trying not to feel overwhelmed inside.

That distinction matters.

Eventually, many people realize that the same technology helping them escape emotionally is also worsening the nervous system dysregulation underneath.

They may feel simultaneously:

- overstimulated
- emotionally empty
- unable to disconnect
- That contradiction defines modern digital burnout.

◈

Children Growing Up Inside the Scroll

This conversation becomes even more urgent when we talk about children.

Many children are growing up in environments shaped by:

- constant stimulation
- pressure toward shorter attention spans
- algorithmic entertainment
- emotional comparison
- digital validation
- nonstop screen exposure

Developing nervous systems are especially vulnerable.

Children need:

- boredom
- imagination
- physical movement
- emotional connection
- face-to-face interaction
- nervous system regulation
- unstructured play

- moments of silence

But modern childhood increasingly removes or reduces those experiences.

Instead, stimulation arrives instantly.

Constantly.

That does not mean technology is evil.

Technology can educate, connect, inspire, and support.

But children's nervous systems still require protection from overstimulation.

They need limits.

They need rhythm.

They need recovery.

They need room to be bored, move, imagine, and connect without a screen competing for their attention.

This is especially important for children with ADHD.

Overstimulation can worsen:

- emotional dysregulation
- sleep problems
- impulsivity
- low frustration tolerance
- attention fragmentation

Parents now face challenges no previous generation has fully experienced.

And many parents are already neurologically exhausted themselves.

That reality requires compassion, too.

◈

Reclaiming Attention

The solution is not to reject technology completely.

Technology is part of modern life.

The real question is:

"How do we use technology without allowing it to consume our nervous systems?"

That requires intentionality.

Boundaries.

Awareness.

Periods of disconnection.

Nervous system regulation.

For many people with ADHD, that may mean practicing:

- screen limits
- structured breaks
- reduced notifications
- mindfulness
- movement
- sleep hygiene
- digital detox periods
- intentional offline time

Not as punishment.

Not as restriction for the sake of restriction.

But as protection.

Because attention is not only about productivity.

Attention is life itself.

What people repeatedly give their attention to can shape:

- emotions
- nervous systems

- relationships
- memory
- identity
- mental health

Perhaps one of the greatest tragedies of the digital age is this:

many people are losing pieces of their lives one distracted moment at a time.

Missing conversations.

Missing connection.

Missing stillness.

Missing presence.

Missing joy.

Missing themselves.

The ADHD nervous system does not need more shame for struggling with distraction in a world professionally engineered to capture attention.

But it does need awareness.

It needs protection. It needs recovery.

Healing may begin the moment people stop asking:

"Why can't I focus?"

and start asking:

"What kind of world is my nervous system trying to survive inside every day?"

That question changes everything.

Because reclaiming attention is not just about using technology less.

It is about returning to life more fully.

CHAPTER FIFTEEN

The Future of the ADHD Mind

AI, Neurodiversity, Psychedelics, Innovation, and the Next Generation of Understanding

◈

The Changing Narrative

For much of modern history, ADHD was described almost entirely through deficits.

Disorder.

Impairment.

Problematic behavior.

Inability to focus.

Disruption.

The conversation centered on what people with ADHD could not do.

Sit still.

Stay organized.

Regulate emotions.

Complete tasks consistently.

Follow routines.

Schools, clinics, workplaces, and families often became focused on measuring dysfunction while overlooking the nervous system underneath the behavior.

But something has begun to shift.

Slowly.

Imperfectly.

The narrative is changing.

Not into fantasy.

Not into the claim that ADHD is easy.

Not into romanticizing suffering.

Into something more honest:

ADHD can involve both struggle and potential within the same nervous system.

That distinction matters.

For decades, many people with ADHD grew up believing they were:

- lazy
- broken
- difficult
- emotionally unstable
- irresponsible
- failures

Now, more people are beginning to understand:

many ADHD nervous systems were not defective.

They were unsupported.

Misunderstood.

Overstimulated.

Shamed.

Forced into systems that were never built for the way they naturally process the world.

And once understanding changes, possibility changes too.

That is what this chapter is ultimately about:

hope grounded in reality.

Not false hope.

Not forced positivity.

Not motivational noise.

Real hope.

The kind built from:

- neuroscience
- compassion
- innovation
- regulation
- advocacy
- research
- human connection

The kind that says:

"Maybe we are only beginning to understand the ADHD brain."

And maybe the future of ADHD is not about making every mind fit the same mold.

Maybe it is about finally building a world wise enough to understand different kinds of minds.

◈

AI-Assisted Living

Artificial intelligence could become one of the most important support tools people with ADHD ever receive.

Not because AI will "fix" ADHD.

But because AI may help compensate for executive dysfunction in ways that were not previously possible.

For many people with ADHD, the struggle is not intelligence.

It is execution.

Remembering.

Organizing.

Prioritizing.

Starting.

Transitioning.

Managing overwhelm.

Maintaining structure inside a dysregulated nervous system.

That is where AI could become transformative.

Imagine:

- intelligent scheduling assistance
- adaptive reminders
- emotional regulation prompts
- executive functioning support
- task breakdown systems
- burnout prediction tools
- personalized learning environments
- real-time organizational support
- ADHD-friendly workflow design

Many people with ADHD already use AI informally for:

- planning
- writing
- structure
- brainstorming
- organization
- emotional processing
- productivity support

And honestly?

That matters.

For decades, many people with ADHD were expected to survive inside systems built around neurotypical executive functioning.

Technology now offers the possibility of adaptation instead of punishment.

With ethical design, privacy protection, and human oversight, that shift could become transformative in education, work, and daily life.

Especially for:

- students
- entrepreneurs
- creatives
- clinicians
- parents
- overwhelmed adults

The future may not be about forcing ADHD minds to function like everyone else.

It may be about building systems that finally support the way ADHD minds actually work.

That possibility is enormous.

◈

The Future of Treatment

The future of ADHD treatment will likely become far more individualized than it has been in the past.

For decades, treatment conversations have often become polarized:

- medication versus no medication
- discipline versus accommodation
- structure versus freedom

But neuroscience increasingly shows that ADHD is complex, varied, and deeply connected to the nervous system.

That means treatment must become more nuanced, too.

The future will likely involve thoughtful combinations of:

- medication
- therapy
- nervous system regulation
- trauma-informed care
- executive functioning support
- lifestyle interventions
- technology-assisted organization
- mindfulness
- coaching
- neurofeedback, when appropriate
- sleep optimization
- personalized treatment planning

And perhaps most importantly:

future treatment may become less shame-based.

That matters profoundly.

Shame has harmed countless people with ADHD.

Especially children.

Especially women.

Especially people in recovery.

Especially outwardly successful adults who are quietly collapsing inside.

Future treatment models must recognize this:

people with ADHD do not simply need symptom suppression.

They need nervous system understanding.

They need support that helps them function without forcing them to disappear inside the treatment plan.

That distinction changes everything.

◈

Psychedelics and Neuroplasticity

One of the most controversial and rapidly evolving areas of mental health research involves psychedelics and psychedelic-assisted therapies.

Psilocybin.

Ketamine.

MDMA-assisted therapy.

LSD microdosing.

The conversation surrounding these substances and treatments has expanded dramatically in recent years.

Especially around:

- trauma
- depression
- addiction
- neuroplasticity
- emotional rigidity
- nervous system healing

Some individuals with ADHD report that psychedelic experiences have helped them:

- feel more emotionally connected
- process trauma
- interrupt destructive patterns
- increase mindfulness
- reduce emotional numbness
- understand themselves differently

Researchers are increasingly exploring whether psychedelic-assisted approaches may influence:

- emotional regulation

- cognitive flexibility
- neural connectivity
- trauma processing
- mood disorders

But this area requires enormous caution and honesty.

The science is still emerging.

The internet often exaggerates early findings.

And psychedelics are not emotionally or medically safe for every nervous system.

This is especially important for individuals with:

- vulnerability to psychosis
- bipolar-spectrum conditions
- unstable substance use
- certain trauma histories
- severe psychiatric instability

This chapter is not about reckless promotion.

It is about intellectual openness.

Historically, many groundbreaking conversations in mental health were dismissed before deeper understanding had a chance to develop.

But openness without caution is not wisdom.

The future requires both:

- scientific curiosity
- ethical responsibility

That balance matters deeply.

Especially in ADHD communities, where desperation for relief can sometimes make people vulnerable to hype.

The future of mental health should never be built on stigma.

But it should not be built on false promises either.

◈

The Neurodiversity Movement

One of the most powerful cultural shifts happening today is the growth of the neurodiversity movement.

This movement challenges the idea that every brain must function identically in order to deserve dignity, accommodation, and respect.

That idea matters profoundly for people with ADHD.

Especially because many have spent their entire lives trying desperately to appear "normal."

The neurodiversity movement does not claim that ADHD carries no struggles.

That misunderstanding appears constantly online.

ADHD can absolutely be disabling for many people.

Instead, the movement argues something deeper:

difference does not automatically equal defectiveness.

That perspective changes the emotional conversation entirely.

Instead of asking:

"How do we force this person to fit the system?"

the question becomes:

"How do we build systems that recognize neurological diversity more humanely?"

That shift affects:

- education
- workplaces
- parenting
- healthcare
- relationships
- mental health treatment

And honestly?

The world may desperately need the strengths many people with ADHD often carry:

- creativity
- innovation
- emotional intensity
- risk tolerance
- divergent thinking
- adaptability
- intuition
- entrepreneurial thinking

Many systems were built around conformity.

But innovation rarely comes from conformity.

It often comes from minds willing to think differently.

◈

What Healing May Look Like

Healing for ADHD individuals may look very different in the future than it has in the past.

For many years, healing was often reduced to symptom management: focusing longer, performing more consistently, and appearing more regulated on the outside.

But true healing may require something deeper.

Nervous system regulation.

Emotional safety.

Reduced shame.

Trauma-informed understanding.

Compassionate accountability.

Adaptive systems.

Supportive environments.

At its best, healing may involve teaching people:

- how to regulate emotions
- how to structure life sustainably
- how to protect nervous system capacity
- how to recognize overstimulation before it becomes collapse
- how to recover from burnout without shame
- how to communicate needs clearly
- how to stop equating productivity with worth

That final shift may become one of the most important of all.

Many ADHD individuals have spent decades trying to earn acceptance through overperformance. They learned to push past exhaustion, mask their needs, and prove their value through output.

Healing may finally help them understand a truth they should never have had to earn:

they were worthy before they proved anything.

For high-functioning adults who survived through masking, chronic self-pressure, and the constant need to appear okay, that realization can change the entire way they relate to themselves.

◈

The Kids Growing Up Right Now

Perhaps the most important part of this future involves children.

Today's children are growing up in a world previous generations were never fully prepared to navigate:

- nonstop stimulation
- social media
- algorithmic attention systems
- digital comparison
- constant accessibility
- educational pressure
- emotional overload

Many ADHD children are not simply distracted. They are growing up in environments that can overstimulate, overwhelm, and exhaust their nervous systems before they even have the language to explain what is happening.

That reality should concern everyone.

But there is also hope.

More parents are learning.

More teachers are learning.

More clinicians are learning.

More adults are beginning to understand emotional regulation, executive dysfunction, masking, rejection sensitivity, and nervous system overload.

This growing awareness matters.

Children growing up today may receive language, support, and validation that many ADHD adults never had. They may learn earlier that their struggles are not character flaws. They may be guided with more compassion, more structure, and more understanding.

A child who can say,

"My nervous system works differently,"

often carries far less shame than a child who silently believes,

"I am defective."

That difference can change the course of a life.

◈

The Next Generation of Understanding

The future of ADHD understanding will likely require one major shift above all others:

moving from judgment toward curiosity.

For too long, many ADHD behaviors have been interpreted through the lens of character, discipline, or personal failure.

Instead of asking:

- "Why are they lazy?"
- "Why can't they focus?"
- "Why are they so emotional?"
- "Why can't they just try harder?"
- the future asks better questions:
- "What is this nervous system experiencing?"
- "What support is missing?"
- "What environment is overwhelming this person?"
- "What strengths exist beneath the dysregulation?"
- "How can this person function without shame?"

That shift may sound simple.

But culturally, it is profound.

Shame-based systems have already failed countless people.

The future requires something different:

- education
- compassion
- evidence-based care
- nervous system awareness
- flexibility
- innovation

And perhaps most importantly, it requires hope.

Real hope.

Not the kind that pretends ADHD is easy.

Not the kind that romanticizes struggle.

Not the kind that ignores the exhaustion behind the brilliance.

But the kind that recognizes a more honest truth:

extraordinary minds can carry extraordinary strengths and extraordinary struggles at the same time.

◈

The Future Is Not About Becoming Normal

Perhaps one of the greatest mistakes many ADHD individuals learned growing up was believing that healing meant becoming "normal."

Quieter.

Less emotional.

More compliant.

More manageable.

Less intense.

Less themselves.

But the future may finally recognize something essential:

many ADHD individuals were never meant to become smaller versions of themselves.

They were meant to become safer, steadier, more supported versions of themselves.

Regulated versions of themselves.

That is different.

The goal is not to destroy intensity.

The goal is to help a person carry intensity safely.

The goal is not to remove emotion.

The goal is to build emotional regulation.

The goal is not to eliminate creativity.

The goal is to protect the nervous system that carries it.

The goal is not to force every electric mind into silence.

The goal is to teach electric minds how to stop burning themselves alive just to survive.

And maybe that is where the future finally begins.

Not with fear.

Not with shame.

Not with the belief that neurodivergence must be erased before a person can be whole.

But with a simple, powerful realization:

people with ADHD were never hopeless.

The world simply misunderstood the electricity inside them for far too long.

CLOSING

Learning to Harness the Storm

For most of his life, he believed the goal was to become normal.

Quieter.

Less emotional.

Less impulsive.

Less intense.

Less distracted.

Less overwhelming.

Less himself.

That is what so many people with ADHD spend years trying to do:

survive by shrinking themselves.

They shrink the emotions.

They shrink the energy.

They shrink the personality.

They shrink the sensitivity.

They shrink the chaos.

They shrink the dreams.

They shrink the intensity.

Because somewhere along the way, many learned a devastating lesson:

"The real you is too much for people."

Too loud.

Too emotional.

Too forgetful.

Too impulsive.

Too difficult.

Too intense.

Too scattered.

Too sensitive.

Too exhausting.

After hearing those messages enough times from schools, relationships, workplaces, systems, and even from inside their own minds, many people with ADHD begin living permanently in survival mode.

Not trying to thrive.

Trying not to fail in public.

Trying not to disappoint people.

Trying not to overwhelm people.

Trying not to fall apart.

That is exhausting.

And perhaps that is one of the greatest tragedies of ADHD:

not the symptoms alone, but the shame people absorb while trying to survive them.

Because shame changes the nervous system.

Shame teaches people:

- “to hide
- “to mask
- “to overperform
- “to apologize constantly
- “to distrust themselves
- “to disconnect from their own needs

Eventually, many people stop asking:

“What do I need to regulate?”

and begin asking:

"How do I become acceptable?"

That question quietly erodes people.

Especially emotionally intense people.

Especially sensitive people.

Especially children.

Especially people recovering from addiction.

Especially high-functioning adults carrying invisible nervous system exhaustion behind polished smiles.

But somewhere inside all that chaos, many people with ADHD also carry extraordinary things.

Vision.

Passion.

Empathy.

Creativity.

Resilience.

Intuition.

Intensity.

Innovation.

The ability to feel deeply.

The ability to connect deeply.

The ability to build, create, dream, fight, survive, and reinvent themselves again and again.

That electricity is real too.

This is where the conversation about ADHD must finally become more honest.

ADHD is not simply a superpower.

That oversimplification hurts people, because many individuals with ADHD have suffered profoundly:

- "addiction
- "burnout

- “anxiety
- “emotional dysregulation
- “relationship struggles
- “shame
- “depression
- “self-doubt
- “nervous system collapse

Some have spent years fighting to survive their own minds.

This book was never written to romanticize suffering.

But ADHD is also not simply a story of brokenness.

That oversimplification hurts people too, because many individuals with ADHD also carry:

- “brilliance
- “emotional depth
- “creativity
- “adaptability
- “innovation
- “fierce empathy
- “extraordinary resilience

The truth lives in the tension between both realities.

ADHD is often a double-edged nervous system.

The same mind that creates chaos can create beauty.

The same intensity that disrupts peace can create purpose.

The same emotional sensitivity that causes suffering can create extraordinary compassion.

The same nervous system that once searched desperately for escape can, with support and healing, become a source of safety for others.

That transformation matters.

Because many people reading this book may still be trapped in survival mode.

Still drowning in shame.

Still exhausted from masking.

Still trying desperately to outrun themselves.

Still believing they are failures because life feels harder for them neurologically than it seems to feel for others.

To those people, this message matters deeply:

You are not lazy.

You are not weak.

You are not broken.

Your nervous system may have spent years overloaded, misunderstood, dysregulated, overstimulated, unsupported, and shamed.

And healing does not begin by hating yourself harder.

Healing begins with understanding.

Understanding:

- "your nervous system
- "your emotional patterns
- "your overstimulation
- "your dopamine-seeking
- "your burnout
- "your shame
- "your trauma
- "your strengths
- "your limits
- "your humanity

Once people begin to understand themselves differently, they often stop fighting themselves so violently.

This is where regulation begins.

Not perfection.

Not emotional numbness.

Not becoming neurotypical.

Regulation.

Safety.

Awareness.

Compassion.

Structure.

Boundaries.

Connection.

Rest.

Support.

And perhaps most importantly, permission to exist without constantly apologizing for how their brain works.

This does not mean avoiding accountability.

ADHD still requires responsibility. People still need:

- "treatment
- "structure
- "emotional regulation
- "honesty
- "support systems
- "boundaries
- "growth

But accountability without shame changes lives.

Compassion without enabling changes lives.

Understanding without minimizing struggle changes lives.

That balance matters.

Especially in a world built around distraction, overstimulation, comparison, urgency, and emotional exhaustion.

Modern life is burning out millions of nervous systems. ADHD nervous systems often burn out faster, not because they are weaker, but because they are carrying more friction in environments that rarely slow down.

So people with ADHD may need to become fiercely intentional about protecting what keeps them steady:

- "sleep
- "peace
- "nervous system capacity
- "emotional safety
- "stillness
- "attention
- "recovery

That is not weakness.

That is wisdom.

That is survival.

Maybe this is the final lesson this book hopes to leave behind:

The goal was never to destroy the storm inside the ADHD mind.

The goal is to understand it, regulate it, and learn how to harness it without letting it destroy you.

Because storms can destroy things.

But storms also carry power.

Electricity.

Movement.

Transformation.

And when that force is understood, supported, regulated, and directed with intention, it can become something more than chaos.

It can become light.

Light for entire rooms.

Light for entire families.

Light for entire communities.

Light for entire lives.

For decades, many people with ADHD have lived believing they were "too much."

Too emotional.

Too distracted.

Too impulsive.

Too intense.

Too sensitive.

Too chaotic.

But perhaps the truth was never that they were too much.

Perhaps no one ever taught them how to carry that much electricity safely.

And maybe that understanding changes everything.

Epilogue

You Were Never Broken

Somewhere tonight, a child with ADHD is lying awake in bed, replaying every moment they got in trouble that day.

Every correction.

Every frustrated look.

Every moment they disappointed someone again.

Their body is exhausted.

Their nervous system is not.

Their mind keeps moving:

- too fast
- too loud
- too emotional
- too awake

And somewhere deep inside that child, a thought begins to form before they even know how to say it aloud:

"Why is being me so hard?"

Somewhere else tonight, a teenager is scrolling endlessly, trying to outrun the feeling that they are falling behind everyone else.

A mother is sitting in her car, crying quietly after another overwhelming day of parenting, secretly wondering if she is failing her child.

A father is losing his temper, then hating himself afterward because he can no longer seem to regulate the pressure building inside his nervous system.

A college student is drowning in executive dysfunction while everyone around them says, "You just need to try harder."

A woman is masking so perfectly at work that nobody sees the panic attacks happening privately in the bathroom.

A person in recovery is sitting in a meeting, trying desperately to explain that substances were never really about partying.

They were about silence.

A high-performing professional is answering emails while privately imagining what it would feel like to disappear from every responsibility, because burnout has hollowed them out emotionally.

And somewhere, maybe for the first time in their life, someone is finally reading words that make them feel understood.

Not judged.

Not weak.

Not dramatic.

Understood.

That matters more than most people realize.

People can survive incredible pain when they feel seen within it.

But isolation?

Shame?

Misunderstanding?

Those things destroy people quietly.

For generations, many individuals with ADHD have suffered in silence because the world misunderstood what ADHD often is.

People saw behaviors.

They missed the nervous systems underneath them.

They saw impulsivity.

They missed emotional flooding.

They saw distraction.

They missed exhaustion.

They saw unfinished tasks.

They missed shame.

They saw emotional reactions.

They missed dysregulation.

They saw addiction.

They missed pain.

They saw burnout.

They missed survival mode.

This book was written because too many people have spent their entire lives believing they were morally failing, when in reality, they were neurologically overwhelmed.

That distinction changes everything.

Once people stop viewing themselves as broken, they can begin healing differently.

Not perfectly.

Differently.

With more compassion.

More honesty.

More sustainability.

The future of ADHD understanding cannot revolve only around symptom control.

It must include nervous system awareness.

Emotional education.

Trauma-informed care.

Executive functioning support.

Burnout prevention.

Reduced shame.

Real conversations.

Honest conversations.

Especially honest conversations about:

- addiction
- rejection sensitivity
- emotional dysregulation
- masking
- overstimulation
- burnout
- high-functioning collapse

Because hiding those realities has never protected people.

It has only isolated them.

And perhaps that isolation is one of the deepest wounds many people with ADHD carry.

The feeling of constantly being:

- misunderstood
- too intense
- too emotional
- too scattered
- too much

For many, that phrase follows them everywhere:

"Too much."

"Too loud."

"Too sensitive."

"Too energetic."

"Too emotional."

"Too passionate."

"Too forgetful."

"Too impulsive."

"Too intense."

Eventually, many people begin shrinking themselves to survive other people's discomfort.

That shrinking is heartbreaking.

Because the same intensity that sometimes overwhelms others is often the same intensity capable of:

- extraordinary creativity
- deep empathy
- innovation
- leadership
- resilience
- healing
- advocacy
- transformation

The world needs emotionally awake people.

It needs creative thinkers.

It needs people willing to challenge systems, innovate, feel deeply, and fight for human connection.

And many ADHD individuals naturally carry those gifts.

But gifts can become dangerous when they are unsupported.

Electricity without grounding burns.

That is the truth.

The answer was never to pretend ADHD is only a superpower.

That minimizes suffering.

And the answer was never to pretend ADHD is only a curse.

That minimizes potential.

The truth is more complicated.

More human.

ADHD can feel beautiful and brutal at the same time.

It can create:

- innovation and exhaustion
- passion and impulsivity
- empathy and emotional flooding

- brilliance and chaos
- connection and overwhelm

The same nervous system can hold all of it.

That complexity is what makes ADHD so difficult to explain to people who have never lived inside it.

And honestly, many people with ADHD are tired of explaining themselves.

Tired of masking.

Tired of apologizing.

Tired of surviving inside systems that were never designed with their nervous systems in mind.

That exhaustion deserves compassion.

Not pity.

Compassion.

Because many ADHD individuals are not weak.

They are overstimulated.

Emotionally overloaded.

Often misunderstood by environments that were never taught how to recognize their needs.

Their nervous systems adapted in order to survive.

And still, despite all of it, many became:

- loving parents
- leaders
- artists
- clinicians
- teachers
- entrepreneurs
- advocates
- survivors

That resilience deserves recognition too.

Especially for people in recovery with ADHD.

Many did not turn toward substances because they were bad, broken, or hopeless. Many were trying desperately to regulate nervous systems they did not yet understand.

They were trying to stop the noise.

Trying to slow the mind.

Trying to quiet emotional pain.

Trying to survive themselves.

And for those individuals especially, this message matters:

your story did not end with your worst coping mechanism.

You are still here.

That matters.

You survived.

And survival becomes even more meaningful when it is transformed into understanding, compassion, advocacy, and healing.

Maybe that is ultimately the real purpose of this book:

Not simply to explain ADHD academically.

But to help people feel less alone inside it.

To help exhausted parents understand their children differently.

To help adults understand themselves with more compassion.

To help clinicians see nervous systems more clearly and more humanely.

To help people in recovery understand the overlap between dopamine, trauma, shame, and survival.

To help high-functioning people recognize burnout before collapse takes everything from them.

To help emotionally intense people realize they are not monsters for feeling deeply.

To help children grow up with less shame than previous generations carried.

Because shame changes lives.

But so does understanding.

And perhaps that is where everything begins to change: the moment someone finally realizes,

"Maybe I was never broken in the first place."

Maybe the child who could not sit still was not defective.

Maybe the teenager drowning in overstimulation was not lazy.

Maybe the woman masking panic behind professionalism was not weak.

Maybe the person in recovery searching for silence was not hopeless.

Maybe the emotionally overwhelmed parent was not failing.

Maybe the nervous system simply needed support instead of punishment.

Compassion instead of humiliation.

Regulation instead of shame.

Understanding instead of judgment.

That possibility changes futures.

And if there is one final truth worth leaving behind, it is this:

People with ADHD do not need the world to fear their intensity anymore.

They need the world to help them learn how to carry it safely.

Because hidden inside many electric minds are people who have spent their entire lives trying not to burn everyone else while quietly burning themselves alive.

And they deserved help long before they deserved shame.

You were never broken.

You were carrying electricity without a map.

www.ingramcontent.com/pod-product-compliance
Lightning Source LLC
LaVergne TN
LVHW090313210926
848480LV00001B/230